the Weekend Crafter

Paper Quilling

Beautiful Paper Filigree to Make in a Weekend

MALINDA JOHNSTON

LARK BOOKS

A Division of Sterling Publishing Co., Inc.
New York

Editor: Chris Rich
Art Director: Elaine Thompson
Photographer: Evan Bracken
Illustrator: Bobby Gold

Library of Congress Cataloging-in-Publication Data
Johnston, Malinda.
     Paper quilling : beautiful paper filigree to make in a weekend /by
Malinda Johnston. -- 1st ed.
          p.   cm. -- (The weekend crafter)
     Includes index.
     ISBN 1-57990-013-5
     1. Paper quillwork.   I. Title.   II. Series
TT870.J663   1998
745.54--DC21   97-24602
                                                               CIP

10 9 8 7 6 5 4 3

Published by Lark Books, a division of
Sterling Publishing Co., Inc.
387 Park Avenue South, New York, N.Y. 10016

The Bouquet design on pages 24-25 is reprinted by permission of *Crafts Magazine*,
PJS Publications, Inc., Peoria, IL, from the May 1995 issue of *Crafts*.

Distributed in Canada by Sterling Publishing,
c/o Canadian Manda Group, One Atlantic Ave., Suite 105
Toronto, Ontario, Canada M6K 3E7

Distributed in Australia by Capricorn Link (Australia) Pty Ltd., P.O.
Box 6651, Baulkham Hills, Business Centre
NSW 2153, Australia

Distributed in the U.K. by:
Guild of Master Craftsman Publications Ltd.
Castle Place 166 High Street, Lewes, East Sussex, England, BN7 1XU
Tel: (+ 44) 1273 477374 Fax: (+ 44) 1273 478606
Email: pubs@thegmcgroup.com
Web: www.gmcpublications.com

If you have questions or comments about this book, please contact:
Lark Books
50 College St.
Asheville, NC 28801
(828) 253-0467

Cover Design by Malinda Johnston

*Fringed flowers: purple and lavender 3" lengths, some
⅜" wide and some ¼" wide*

*Eccentric teardrop flowers: purple and lavender 3"
lengths, ⅛" wide, for both teardrops and tight-circle
centers*

*Teardrop flowers: yellow 2" teardrops, ⅛" wide; gold 2"
narrow tight-circle centers*

*Cut-out, fringed leaves: ⅜"-wide lengths of gold quill trim
and two shades of green*

*Looped leaves: green 4¾" lengths, ⅛" wide (pattern on
page 17)*

Stems: green ⅛"-wide lengths

*Butterfly body: Gold quill trim triangle, 4" by ¾", rolled
into bead*

*Wing: Soft yellow 6" and 4" teardrops, ⅛" wide, outlined
with gold quill trim*

Antennae: Two slivers black paper glued together

Contents

Introduction

What is paper quilling? Imagine sitting at your kitchen table. In front of you are some narrow strips of colored paper; a tool that looks like a hat pin with a handle, and a small bottle of craft glue.

You pick up a strip of paper and roll it around the tip of the tool to make a tightly coiled circle. After letting the coils expand a bit, you glue down the loose paper end. Next, you pinch the loosely coiled circle to make a teardrop shape. Then you create four more identical shapes and glue them together in a circle, with their pointed ends facing in. You've just made your first quilled flower.

This is quilling at its simplest: the craft of arranging rolled and shaped strips of paper to make designs. At its most complex, quilling (or paper filigree) is an art form, one that has fascinated people for hundreds of years. During the Renaissance, cloistered nuns decorated reliquaries with elaborate quillwork. Colonial North Americans used quilling to embellish sconces and tea caddies. Even furniture was decorated with quillwork. Today, contemporary quillers make a huge variety of designs: from exquisite framed art to wearable jewelry, decorated boxes, gift cards, and more.

Paper quilling is a craft that invites newcomers with open arms. All it takes to learn every basic technique, from rolling different shapes to scrolling, fringing, looping, and weaving paper is a single weekend, a few inexpensive tools, a package of quilling paper, and this book. Within these pages, you'll find complete quilling instructions, helpful photos, and more than 20 beautiful patterns for framed designs, ornaments, jewelry, gift cards, and more.

Before long, you'll be displaying your custom quillwork with pride, making special quilled gifts for friends and family, and sharing new techniques and design concepts with other paper-filigree crafters. Welcome to the wonderful world of paper quilling!

Learning the Basics

By the time you've finished this chapter, you'll know almost everything there is to know about quilling: what quilling paper is and how to purchase it; which tools you'll need and how to use them; and—most important—how to make the many paper shapes that are assembled to make finished quilled designs.

REQUIRED TOOLS AND SUPPLIES

Everything that a beginning quiller needs, except for patience and practice, will fit inside a single drawer. If you're just beginning this wonderful craft, a few basic tools and supplies (they're all described in this section) will get you off to a great start.

Quilling paper

Quilling tool (select one)

    Needle tool

    Slotted quilling tool

    Old-fashioned hat pin

Quilling work board

Ruler

Straight pins

Small, sharp-pointed scissors

Clear-drying, white craft glue

Tissues

Patterns

Pencil

Tracing paper

Quilling Paper

Today, rather than cutting their own paper strips, quillers usually buy packages of precut, high-quality paper strips from quilling suppliers or craft shops. The strips are usually 24 inches in length and come in a wide range of colors and a number of widths, including narrow (slightly wider than $\frac{1}{16}$ inch), $\frac{1}{8}$ inch, $\frac{1}{4}$ inch, and $\frac{3}{8}$ inch. Wider strips ($\frac{1}{2}$ inch and $\frac{5}{8}$ inch) are also available, but these are usually used to make cutouts, fringed flowers, and twisted loops rather than rolls.

The strips in each package are bonded together at both ends with a padding compound. To detach a strip from a package, just pull away its ends. Then tear away a bit from each end of the strip so that none of the bonding material remains. Don't use scissors to cut away the ends; the torn ends of rolled strips can be glued down much more smoothly than cut ones.

Another type of quilling paper, known as metallic quill trim, comes in strips that are silver or gold colored on one surface. These strips make fine fringed flowers and bell shapes. Parchment quilling paper, in several pastel shades, is also available.

Storing quilling paper without wrinkling or twisting it can be quite a challenge. Some quillers make small wooden stands resembling trees, with horizontal "branches" over which they hang the strips. Other quillers keep their strips intact in narrow, handmade cardboard boxes, each about 3 inches by 3 inches by 25 inches.

Tip

❖ Quilling paper of good quality will resist fading, but your paper and finished projects will retain their colors longer if you keep them out of direct sunlight.

Quilling Tools

Quillers used to roll their paper strips around feather quills or hat pins. Hat pins work fine, but today, two special quilling tools are available. One—the needle tool—looks like a hat pin set into a narrow wooden handle. The other—the slotted quilling tool—has a narrow slot at the end of its needle portion, which catches and holds one end of the paper strip as you roll it.

Each tool has its advantages and disadvantages. If you roll your paper strips on the tip of a tapered needle tool, the holes in their centers will be barely visible. Needle tools are also handy as glue applicators. (You'll need to wipe remaining glue from the tip of the tool every time you use it this way.) A slotted quilling tool leaves a larger hole in each paper roll and makes a visible kink in the very end of each paper strip, but this tool can be somewhat easier to handle.

Quilling Work Board

A quilling work board is simply a pattern-holding board that quillers use for assembling projects. Commercial work boards, available from quilling suppliers, consist of flat, cork sheets, usually ⅜ inch thick, that come with clear plastic covers. The project pattern is slipped under the plastic, the paper shapes are arranged on top and held in place with straight pins, and the shapes are glued together. (The cork must be thick enough to hold the straight pins securely.)

To make a quilling work board by hand, cover the smooth side of a sheet of corrugated cardboard with a piece of white paper. Then set your pattern on the white paper and tape a sheet of clear plastic or waxed paper over it.

Tip

- Sometimes glued shapes stick to the plastic on the quilling work board. Carefully slide your needle tool under the quilling to loosen it.

Ruler

The project instructions in this book usually specify how long each strip of paper should be, so a ruler is indispensable. On page 80, you'll find two printed rulers, including one for metric measurements.

Straight Pins

Straight pins are used to hold your quilled shapes in place over the pattern on your quilling work board as you glue the shapes together. You'll also use pins when you make eccentric loose circles and huskings (see pages 12 and 13).

Scissors

You'll need small scissors with sharp, pointed blades for trimming away excess paper, for cutting intricate shapes, and for cutting fringes in strips of paper.

Craft Glue and Tissues

Use a craft glue (not a woodworking or household repair glue) that is colorless when it dries. You don't want the glue to show in your finished projects.

To apply the glue, first squeeze a few drops from the bottle onto a small square of paper. Then dip the tip of a needle tool or a toothpick into these drops and apply a tiny amount (just enough to do the job) to the strip of quilling paper. Wipe your applicator on a piece of tissue every time you use it, or a hardened blob of glue will develop on its end.

Tip

> ◆ Never use more glue than necessary when making quilled shapes and assembling the shapes into finished projects. Remember, too, that when you assemble your projects, shapes with glue on one surface should be positioned face down.

Patterns

Building a collection of patterns, both purchased and self-designed, is a great way to make sure you never run out of projects that please you. To keep the originals from being marred, trace them, file away the originals, and use the traced copies as you work.

Patterns vary from project to project. Many show the entire design. These are used both to make the individual shapes and to assemble the shapes into a finished project. Other patterns show the individual parts of the finished project separately. You'll make each part on its pattern and

then use the project photo or an illustration of the overall design as an assembly guide.

Sometimes, you'll run into a pattern that shows only one-half of a symmetrical project. The Filigree Medallion on page 58 is an excellent example. First, use tracing paper to make a copy of the half-pattern provided. Then flip the tracing over, align it with the original, and trace the other half to make a full, traced pattern.

Assembly methods also differ. Sometimes, it's best to glue individual shapes together as you create them. This way, you don't have to worry about a table top cluttered with tiny shapes, and you can also adjust shapes to fit your pattern outline as you fill it in.

At other times, it's best to make all the shapes first and then glue them together. This method allows you to select perfectly matched shapes from among the many you've made—a real advantage when you want to create a teardrop flower, for example, with identical teardrop petals.

Tip

> ◆ When working with symmetrical projects, always start assembling the shapes from the center of the pattern and work your way out toward the pattern's edges.

OPTIONAL TOOLS AND SUPPLIES

Once you're sure that you'd like to continue quilling, you'll definitely want to add a few more tools and supplies to your beginner's collection.

  Quilling/designer board

  Compass

  Protractor

  Graph paper

  Fine-pointed tweezers

  Fringing tool

Quilling/Designer Board

A specialty item available from quilling suppliers, this inexpensive board is basically a sheet of corkboard, one side of which contains circular molds in six different sizes and a triangular area for keeping your straight pins handy. The molds, which accommodate 3-, 6-, 9-, 12-, 15-, and 18-inch lengths of rolled paper, are used to shape uniformly sized loose circles and eccentric loose circles (see pages 10 and 12 for details). The bare cork back can be covered with waxed paper or plastic and used as a quilling work board for assembling finished projects.

Tip

> ◆ By all means experiment with the molds in the quilling/designer board. You'll find that using shorter strips of paper in them produces loose circles that are quite open, while longer strips yield loose circles that are denser.

Compass, Protractor, and Graph Paper

When you're designing symmetrical projects such as the one shown in the photo above, a special pattern is required. Start by using a compass to draw several, equidistant concentric circles on a sheet of graph paper. Then, using a protractor and ruler, divide the circles into equal segments. By slipping this pattern behind the plastic on your quilling work board and using its lines and circles as guides, you'll end up with design parts that are perfectly aligned.

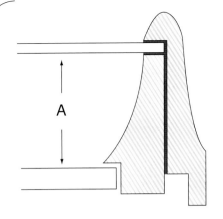

Tweezers

Tweezers with very fine points will come in handy when you need to arrange tiny quilled shapes during project assembly, adjust the coils in a loose circle or eccentric shape, and rearrange stray fringes on fringed flowers.

Fringing Tool

Fringing is the process of cutting tiny slits along one edge of a paper strip. You can cut these with scissors or you can use a fringing tool, available from quilling suppliers. The tool works well with ¼-inch- and ⅜-inch-wide paper, but ⅛-inch-wide paper must be fringed

by hand. You'll find that the tool is much easier to use if you use screws to secure it to a small board or to your permanent work surface.

Tip

➤ Glass-covered shadow boxes, which are basically just deep, two-part frames, lend finished quillwork a special depth as well as protecting it from dust. Framers make these boxes by combining two different moldings. The illustration (above right) shows a typical example, with one molding that flares outward at the top, the quillwork beneath it, and another, exterior molding to hold the glass in place on top. When selecting

shadow-box moldings, make sure that the distance between your quillwork and the glass (dimension A) is appropriate. Quillwork with only one layer of narrow paper, for example, looks best when the recess in the box is relatively shallow.

TECHNIQUES AND SHAPES

Finished quillwork consists of individual quilled shapes, most made from narrow strips of paper. Some of these shapes are standard, and others are spontaneously designed by individual

Rolls

Scrolls

Eccentric Rolls

quillers as they work. In this section, you'll find descriptions of the common standard shapes, as well as instructions for making them. Practice before you tackle your first project, using 4-inch lengths of ⅛-inch-wide paper. (Remember to tear your paper to length rather than cutting it!)

Rolls

All rolls are started by using a quilling tool to roll a strip of quilling paper.

Tight Circle

This very simple shape is often used to make flower centers.

Moisten one end of your paper strip slightly and position that end flat against your index finger. Place the needle portion of your needle tool flat against the paper end at a 90-degree angle, and use your thumb to press the paper around the tool.

Hold the tool stationary and roll the paper carefully around it to form a tight coil. Be sure to keep the paper edges even. When you're finished, slip the needle tool out from the coil's center, holding the coil together with your fingers.

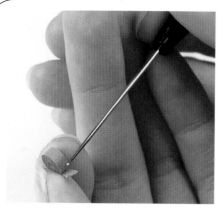

Using the tip of your needle tool or a toothpick, apply a tiny dab of glue to the loose, torn end of the paper strip. Then press the gluey end down to secure it, holding it in place until the glue does its job. Always wipe the tip of your needle tool clean after each glue application.

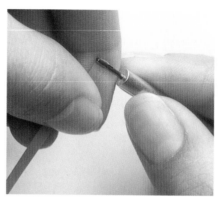

You may also use a slotted quilling tool to make tight circles. Just thread one end of the paper strip into the slot, making sure that the edge of the strip is at the very end of the slot. Then turn the tool while you maintain some tension on the paper strip.

Tip

> If you're a beginner, use the center of your tapered needle tool rather than its tip. When you've had some practice, use the tapered tip; it will leave a smaller hole in the center of the roll.

Loose Circle

This quilling shape can be transformed, by pinching it, into many other unique shapes, so it's very common indeed. First roll a tight circle. Then, before gluing the

loose end down, let the coils relax so that the circle expands. (You can use the tip of your needle tool to adjust the space between the coils.) Once expansion is complete, glue the end in place.

Tip

> A quilling/designer board comes in handy when you want to make a series of matched loose circles.

Teardrop

Pinch one side of a glued loose circle to form a point.

Shaped Teardrop

Curl the point of a teardrop.

Marquise

Pinch opposite sides of a loose circle into points.

Shaped Marquise

Curl the two pinched points of a marquise in opposite directions.

Crescent

Pinch two points on a loose circle, but make sure the points aren't exactly opposite one another. Then curl the points toward each other.

Square

Make a marquise. Then turn it 90 degrees and pinch two more points on opposite sides.

Rectangle

Make a marquise, turn it just slightly, and pinch two more points on opposite sides.

Triangle

Pinch three points on a loose circle by pressing the circle

between the thumb and index finger of one hand while pushing it against the flat of one finger on the other hand.

Bunny Ear

Make this just as you would a crescent, but position the points closer together.

Half Circle

Pinch a loose circle at two points to form one flat surface.

Rolled Heart (or Arrow)

Make a teardrop and create a sharp indentation in the rounded end.

Holly Leaf

Pinch six points on a loose circle. Then make rounded indentations between each pair of points.

Scrolls

Unlike rolls, scrolls don't form solid shapes. They're made by rolling one or both ends of a paper strip, and one end is often left unglued.

Loose Scroll

Roll only a portion of the paper strip, leaving an unglued tail at the end.

Open Heart

Make a crease in the center of the paper strip. Then roll each end inward toward the crease.

V Scroll

Crease the paper strip at the center and roll each end outward. (To make a closed V scroll, just glue together the flat inner surfaces of the V.)

S Scroll

Roll each end of the strip towards the center to form an S shape.

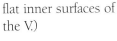

C Scroll

Roll each end of the strip towards the center to make a C shape.

Scroll Variations

Scrolls can be varied in a number of ways, including folding the paper off-center and doubling the paper lengths.

Off-Center Scrolls

The four scroll variations shown are simply scrolls that have been rolled off-center.

Double Scroll

Place two lengths of paper, one shorter than the other, on top of each other, with one end of the shorter length about $\frac{1}{4}$ inch from one end of the longer length. Glue these overlapping ends together. Then, starting from the end that has the longer strip on the outside, roll the strips together. Allow the coiled strips to relax; then tug slightly on the shorter length to separate the coils. Glue the ends together.

Double Scroll with Flag

Fold a paper strip in half; then roll it, starting with the loose, overlapped ends. The inner strip will bulge to form a flag near the crease.

Triple Scroll

Fold a paper strip in half; then roll each loose end for a few turns. Roll the folded end down as shown in the photo.

Connected Scrolls

Curve the unrolled ends of several loose scrolls away from their rolled portions. Then form a row of scrolls by gluing each curved end to the rolled end of another scroll.

Eccentric Shapes

Eccentric shapes are made with loose circles, the centers of which have been pulled toward one edge and glued in place.

Eccentric Loose Circle

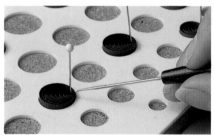

Make a loose circle, using a quilling/designer board, and glue its loose outer end. Then use a straight pin to pull its center to the mold's edge and push the pin into the board. To hold the center in place permanently, apply a tiny dab of glue to the paper coils between the straight pin and the edge of the mold. Remove the pin when the glue has dried, twisting it slightly to loosen any glue stuck to it.

Eccentric Teardrop and Eccentric Marquise

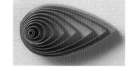

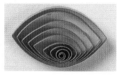

Shape these just as you would when making teardrops and marquises from ordinary loose circles.

Eccentric Fan

Hold the points of an eccentric marquise with the thumb and index finger. Then press inward on the same side of each point to expand the coils on one side of the marquise.

Eccentric Crescent and Eccentric Bunny Ear

Shape these just as you would when making crescents and bunny ears from ordinary loose circles.

Eccentric Tulip

On an eccentric marquise, pinch another point on one surface. Indent the two areas between each set of points; then push the three points together.

OTHER SHAPING TECHNIQUES

Looping

Using a single strip of paper, first make a small circle at one end and glue it closed. Continue to make more loops, each slightly larger than the last, pinching each one to a point and gluing it in place before making the next loop.

Making Pegs

Pegs are simply tight circles that are glued to the backs of design sections to raise them above the background. To make double pegs, just glue the bottom of one peg to the top of another.

Making Fringed Flowers

Start by fringing a paper strip, using a fringing tool or scissors. Next, roll the fringed strip into a tight circle and glue down its loose end. Spread out the fringes with one fingernail. You can then curl the outer fringes by using the side of your needle tool.

Making Fringed Flowers with Centers

Select two different widths of paper and fringe the wider one. Make a longer strip by gluing the two strips together. Starting with the narrower paper, roll the glued strip into a tight circle; the narrow strip will form a center for the fringed flower. When you've finished rolling, glue the loose end of the wider strip in place and spread the fringes with your fingernail.

Making Duo-Toned Fringed Flowers

Pick two different colors of paper, each the same width. Fringe both; then place one on top of the other. Roll the doubled strips into a tight circle, glue down the ends, and spread the fringes.

Making Grape Rolls

Push the center of a tight circle outward to form a gently shaped cone. To help the cone keep its shape, spread a thin layer of glue over the surface that will be positioned face down in your finished project.

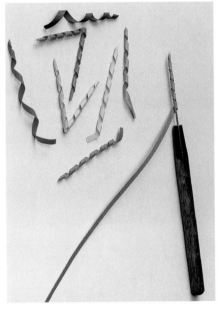

Making Spirals

Place one end of the paper strip at an angle against the quilling tool, not at its tip but next to the handle. Roll the

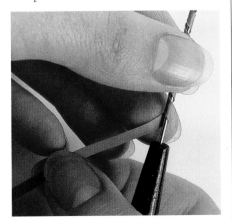

strip, maintaining some tension on the paper with your tool-holding hand, so that the spiral's starting point moves toward the tip of the tool. When the spiral reaches the tip, allow its starting point to slip off the needle so that you can continue spiraling.

To make a loose spiral, rather than a tight one, first make a tight spiral. Then run the side of the needle down the inside of the spiral from its loose to its tight end, as if you were curling a length of ribbon with a scissors' blade. Be sure to stop before you get all the way to the tight end, or you'll take the tension out of the spiral's point. To make V-shaped double spirals, just roll the paper strip from each end.

Making Huskings

Huskings are made by shaping paper around a series of upright straight pins. Straight huskings often serve as flower petals in floral designs. Using the illustrations at the top of the page as guides, insert five straight pins into your quilling work board. Wrap a paper strip around pins 1 and 2 and glue the paper together where the strip overlaps at pin 1. Continue by wrapping the strip around pins 3, 4, and 5, as shown. Tear off any excess paper and glue the end in place at pin 1. You may leave the loops rounded or pinch them as desired. Note that straight huskings may also be varied by using different numbers of pins and by placing them at different distances.

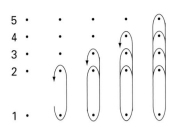

The illustrations below show the pin placement and winding pattern for a fan-shaped husking. For extra strength, make two wraps around pins 1 and 2 when you start and glue the strip to itself in several locations. Before you remove the pins, be sure to apply a bit of glue at the pin 1 position. And remember that if you're making matching huskings, you must reinsert the pins into the same holes after making each one.

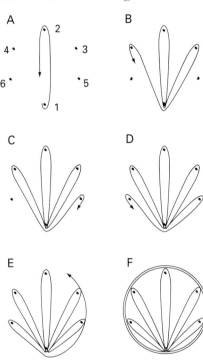

To vary fan-shaped huskings, just rearrange or vary the number of pins.

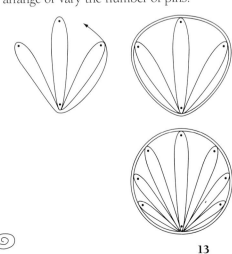

Weaving

Insert a piece of graph paper under the plastic on your quilling work board. Using the graph lines as guides, position several lengths of paper horizontally and pin one end of each in place. Then weave vertical strips under and over them, gluing the strips together every time a horizontal strip crosses a vertical one. Trim the completed weaving as desired.

Tip

➤ To make a solid weaving, butt the edges of the paper strips together so that there's no space between them.

Making Folded Roses

To make the center of the rose, begin rolling a paper strip on a slotted quilling tool. Then fold the paper away from you, at a right angle. Roll the strip again, keeping its bottom edge tight against the tool but allowing its upper edge to flare. Roll until the fold is at the top, make another

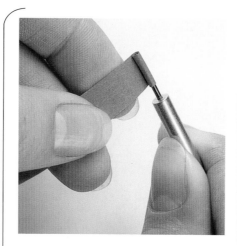

right-angle fold, and roll again, flaring the paper at the top. Repeat until the rose is the desired size; then glue the end in place.

Making Curled Flowers with Paper Rectangles

To make each petal, start by trimming a piece of ⅜-inch-wide paper to ½ inch in length. Using the side of your quilling tool, curl the two corners at one narrow end and cut a slit in the other end. Turn the paper so the curled corners face down; then overlap and glue together the two sections at the slit end. Repeat to make a total of ten petals. Glue the overlapped ends of five petals together to form the inner circle of petals. Create the outer petal layer by gluing the remaining petals underneath the inner petals. To add a flower center, roll a small tight or loose circle and glue it into the center of the flower.

Quilling
Designs

As you'll soon discover, individual quilled designs are as different from one another as the quillers who create them. In fact, the range of contemporary quillwork is phenomenal—from realistic to abstract, whimsical to elegant, and decorative to functional. In this section, you'll find more than 20 projects, all carefully selected to demonstrate some of the many different ways in which quilling enthusiasts work.

If you're a newcomer to quilling, start with the first few projects in this section: The Butterfly, Wreath, and Gift Cards. These small, attractive designs will give you plenty of practice making and assembling the most commonly used standard shapes. By the time you've finished, you'll be ready to tackle any project that catches your fancy.

Starting Tips

- Take the time to read the project instructions carefully. They'll let you know what widths of paper to use, how long each piece should be, what shapes to make, and how to assemble your design.

- The instructions usually specify paper colors, too, but these recommendations aren't written in stone. By all means substitute other colors if you like.

- Be gentle on yourself! Quilling is one of those crafts that you learn with your hands as well as your head. If the petals of your first eccentric teardrop flower aren't perfectly matched, relax, display your slightly lopsided first attempt with a grin, and move on. Your hands will learn more quickly if you don't get impatient with them.

- Don't hesitate to create your own designs. You don't need an art degree to be a creative quiller. Make a few sketches, turn the one you like best into a pattern, and experiment by using different paper shapes.

Wreath and Gift Cards

Once you know how to make the standard shapes, quilling is an incredibly versatile craft, as these simple but lovely projects clearly demonstrate.

(The gift cards are shown on the following page.)

Tips

- Use ⅛-inch-wide paper unless another width is specified. (You can complete all these small projects with a single multicolored package of ⅛-inch-wide paper and a few ⅜-inch lengths.)

- Colors aren't specified in these projects; just use any you like. When making gift cards, you may want to select colors that match or complement your gift wrap.

- Because many of the shapes in these small projects are identical, the instructions presented here are somewhat different in form from the instructions for other projects in this book. Every basic shape is described and illustrated; just make the ones that appear in your selected project and use the photos as guides when gluing the shapes in place.

Teardrop Flower

Make five 3-inch teardrops and glue them together as shown. To make a flower center, roll a 2-inch loose circle and glue it on top of the teardrop petals. To add scrolls to these flowers, use 1-inch lengths, rolling one end of each into a loose circle.

Bunny Ear Flower

Make four 3-inch bunny ears and glue them together. Add a 3-inch tight circle as a flower center, gluing it on top of the petals.

Marquise Flower

Glue six 3-inch marquises together as shown. Then add a 3-inch tight circle on top as a flower center.

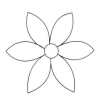

Looped Leaf

Mark a 4¾-inch length of paper as shown in the illustration. Then shape the length

¾"   1"   1¼"   1"   ¾"

into loops, creasing the paper at the marks and gluing each loop as you form it.

Fringed Flower

Glue a 3-inch length of $\frac{1}{8}$-inch-wide paper to a 3-inch length of fringed $\frac{3}{8}$-inch-wide paper, end to end. Then roll this 6-inch length into a tight circle and curl the fringes outward. (Note that the fringed flowers in the Bouquet Card design are made with $\frac{3}{8}$-inch-wide gold quill trim.)

Teardrop Leaf (in Wreath Design)

For each leaf, make a 3-inch teardrop. Glue the leaves between the flower petals after gluing the flowers to the background so that you can position some leaves at upward angles.

Bow (in Wreath Design)

Make fifteen loops, using lengths that range from $1\frac{1}{2}$ to $1\frac{3}{4}$ inches. To make the short streamers, loosely curl one end of each of five short lengths. (When you assemble the wreath, add the bow last, positioning and gluing each loop and streamer one by one.)

Bee (in Horizontal Floral Design)

The bee's head is a 4-inch tight circle. To make the antennae, just fold a very short length into a V shape and glue it to the head. The body is a 4-inch teardrop, and the wings are 3-inch teardrops.

Stems and Scrolls (in Vertical Bouquet Design)

Use short lengths as stems. To make the three scrolls, roll a loose circle at one end of a 2-inch length, a 2½-inch length, and a 3½-inch length.

Ribbon and Fringed Leaf
(in Double Flower Design)

Make each ribbon by gluing a ⅛-inch-wide length on top of a ⅜-inch-wide length. (Note the ⅜-inch-wide gold quill trim in the photo.) To make each leaf, cut a leaf shape from ⅝-inch-wide paper and fringe each edge with scissors.

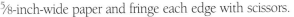

Layered Marquise Flower
(in Double Flower Design)

For each flower, glue together six 4-inch marquise petals. Then glue one flower on top of the other as shown and add a 3-inch tight circle as a flower center.

Bell and Bow (in Bell Design)

For each bell, make a 24-inch grape roll, shaping it so that its narrow end is almost pointed. Then, to make the clapper, roll a 2-inch tight circle, glue it to a short length of narrow paper, and glue the narrow paper inside the bell. To create the bow, first make four individual loops: two with 2-inch lengths and two with 1½-inch lengths. Glue these to the background first. Add two 2-inch tight circles as knots and two short lengths (each slightly curled) as streamers.

Butterfly

At last, a butterfly that enjoys living indoors! Frame this lovely project and display it on any wall in your home, or—if you feel generous— attach the cheerful creature to a gift card, pack the card carefully, and mail it to a special friend.

Tips

+ Use ⅛-inch-wide paper throughout.

+ To make an open-winged butterfly, use the entire butterfly pattern. If you'd rather make a close-winged butterfly, use only one half of the pattern, creating both wings over it. Why? Because glue sometimes shows on the surface of a project that faces the quilling work board during assembly. If you use both sides of the pattern and then flip one wing over to place above the other, unsightly glue may mar your finished project.

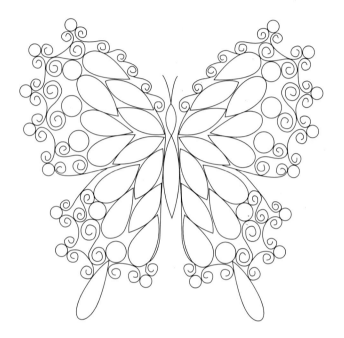

Body and Head

Using the triangular patterns provided, cut the body and head shapes from a sheet of gold paper. Roll each triangle tightly from its wide end and glue the pointed end down. Be sure to keep each roll straight; the point should be in the center when you're finished.

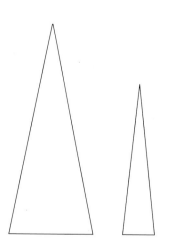

Wings (make two)

For each wing, first roll five yellow 5-inch marquises and glue them together over the pattern. Add seven bright yellow 6-inch teardrops, two gold 2-inch loose circles, and three gold 3-inch loose circles. Roll five bright yellow 3-inch S scrolls and glue these in place as well.

To make the tail at the bottom of the wing, shape a loosely rolled, slender, bright yellow 6-inch teardrop. Glue a length of brown paper around it; then glue the shape in position.

At the upper, inner edge of the wing, glue a row of four brown 1-inch connected scrolls. Then glue a brown 2-inch S scroll to the last connected scroll. Cover the inside edge of the wing, from the first connected scroll down to the wing bottom, with a length of brown paper that has a small loose scroll on one end.

On the outer edge of the wing, in the V where the wing sections separate, glue two short lengths of brown paper, each with a loose scroll on one end. Add seven brown 3-inch C scrolls around the outer edges of the wings. Roll eight brown 1-inch loose circles and glue them to the C scrolls as shown.

Assembly (Butterfly with Open Wings)

Glue the wings to the sides of the body, positioning each one at a slight upward angle. To keep the wings elevated, add two pegs under each one. Make the antennae by cutting two small ⅜-inch-long slivers of gold paper. Cut a point on one end of each and glue the other ends together. Curl the pointed ends slightly and glue the antennae to the top of the head.

Assembly (Butterfly with Closed Wings)

Glue one wing to the body section. When the glue has dried completely, glue the other wing to the body, positioning it at an angle over the lower wing. (The wings should be about ¾ inch apart at their outer edges.) To stabilize the upper wing, glue two or three yellow pegs between the two wings. Make the antennae (see the paragraph just before this one) and glue them in place.

Poppies and Daisies

Why wait for summer to enjoy dazzling white daisies and dashing red poppies? Place this floral arrangement on a bedroom wall and wake up to the special sights of summer every day of the year

Tip

‣ Use narrow paper unless another width is specified.

Poppy Centers *(make three)*

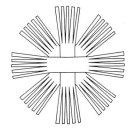

Begin making each center by cutting two ¾-inch lengths of soft green ⅛-inch-wide paper and fringing their ends. Glue these two pieces together in a cross shape as shown. Next, roll a grape roll, using a 6-inch length of ⅛-inch-wide black paper. Glue the grape roll to the center of the cross; then curl the fringed ends up and over it.

Cut four 1¼-inch lengths of ⅛-inch-wide black paper and fringe the ends. Glue these four pieces together as shown. Next, glue the grape roll with soft green fringes in the center of the fringed black paper. Curl the black fringed paper up around the soft green fringes, then curl the very tips of the black fringes away from the soft green fringes.

Large and Medium Poppies (*make one of each*)

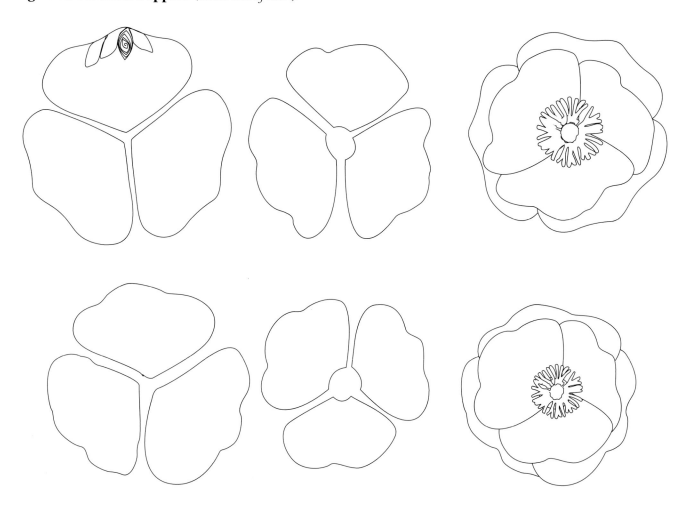

Fill in each set of six petal patterns with red 3-inch marquises. When the glue has dried, gently curve and round each petal by holding it in your palm (front surface up) and pressing it gently with the fingers of your other hand.

Assemble the petals in two layers. Glue the three upper petals to the poppy center first, overlapping them to form a bowl around it. Glue the three lower petals beneath the upper petals, overlapping them as well.

Partly Open Poppy

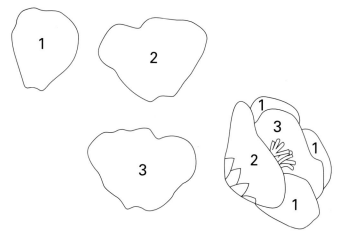

Fill in the petal patterns with red 3-inch marquises, making three petals #1 and one each of petals #2 and #3. When the glue has dried, curve and round each petal as before. Then glue the petals together around a poppy center as shown.

Cut four short pointed lengths of green ⅛-inch-wide paper and curl their pointed ends. Glue these to the base of the flower, on its upper surface, as a calyx.

Large Daisy

To make the daisy center, roll a grape roll from a 15-inch length of gold ⅛-inch-wide paper. Also roll approximately twenty-five white 6-inch teardrops, making each one quite slender. Using the illustration as a guide, glue  half of the petals to the daisy center to form the lower layer and the other half above them to form the upper layer. Be sure to position several petals at angles and to glue most with their outer ends raised.

Small Daisies (make four)

To make each center, roll a grape roll, using a 12-inch length of gold ⅛-inch-wide paper. Roll approximately twenty white 4½-inch teardrops, making these quite slender as well, and assemble as before.

Large Daisy Bud

To make the calyx, roll a green 12-inch grape roll. Then, using 5-inch lengths of white paper, roll ten narrow teardrops for petals and glue their pointed ends into the grape roll.

Small Daisy Buds (make three)

To make all three buds, first roll three green 7-inch grape rolls to serve as calyxes. Using 4-inch lengths of white paper, roll sixteen narrow teardrops for the petals. Glue six petals into one calyx and five into each of the other calyxes.

Large Leaves (make twelve)

For each leaf, roll five green 4-inch marquises, two green 5-inch marquises, and two green 6-inch marquises. Glue together as shown in the illustration.

Medium Leaves (make seven)

For each leaf, roll five green 4-inch marquises and two green 5-inch marquises. Glue the shapes together as shown.

Small Leaves (make six)

To make each leaf, glue together five green 4-inch marquises as shown.

Stems (make four)

For each stem, roll a spiral, using a green length of ⅛-inch-wide paper.

Assembly

Using the photograph on page 21 as a guide, position the three poppies and glue them to the background. Add a stem to the partly open poppy. Glue several large leaves in place around the poppies, making sure to elevate their ends.

Glue a peg made of gold paper to the back of each daisy. Position the daisies and glue them in place. Arrange and glue the remaining leaves, buds, and stems.

Bouquet on a Woven Background

On its elegant woven background, this classic spring bouquet will enhance any room in your home. If you'd like to start with an even easier design, use the gift-tag instructions that come at the end of this project.

Tips

- Use ⅛-inch-wide paper unless another width is specified.
- A quilling/designer board will help you make perfectly matched petals for the teardrop flowers.
- The frame opening shown in the bouquet photo is 7 inches by 8½ inches.

Teardrop Flowers *(make three)*

To make each of the five petals, first glue together a light blue 4-inch length and a turquoise 3-inch length, end to end. Roll the length on a quilling tool, beginning with the light blue end. After allowing the circle to expand in the second smallest mold on the quilling/designer board, shape it into an eccentric teardrop.

Glue the teardrop petals together at their pointed ends. To make the flower center, roll a teal 6-inch grape roll and glue it on top of the petals. Finally, using the photo as a guide, add a 5-inch length of celadon green paper for a stem.

Bunny Ear Flowers *(make five)*

For each flower, first make the stem by rolling a small scroll at one end of a 7-inch length of celadon green paper. Roll three coral 1½-inch tight circles; then glue them to the scrolled end of the stem as shown.

Using lengths of coral paper, roll two 2½-inch bunny ears, two 3-inch bunny ears, and two 3½-inch bunny ears. Glue these to the stem, placing the smallest ones closest to the tight circles and positioning some at slight angles. Roll a celadon green 1-inch loose scroll and glue it to the stem as shown.

Leaves *(make twenty)*

Cut a leaf shape from celadon green ⅜-inch-wide paper. Score its length, fold it in half, and use scissors to fringe its edges.

Leaf Stems (make four)

From celadon green paper, cut four 5-inch lengths. Glue six leaves to each of two lengths. Set these stems aside. Glue three leaves to each of the other two lengths; then roll a loose scroll at the opposite end of each of these two lengths. Glue one leaf to the stem of the center teardrop flower. (You'll add the last leaf to the center teardrop flower after arranging the bouquet.)

Bow with Streamers

To make the bow, first cut a 4½-inch length of ¼-inch-wide soft ivory paper. Then form two loops by gluing its ends back onto its center. Glue a length of ⅛-inch-wide gold quill trim along the center of the glued strip. (Your bow will be smoother if you shape the ¼-inch-wide length into a bow before adding the gold quill trim.)

To form the center of the bow, glue a ½-inch length of ¼-inch-wide soft ivory paper around it. Add a ½-inch length of ⅛-inch-wide gold quill trim around the center of this section.

To make each of the two streamers, first glue a ⅛-inch-wide length of gold quill trim to a 1½-inch length of soft ivory ¼-inch-wide paper. Snip a V into one end of each streamer, curl the ends slightly, and glue the streamers to the bow.

Woven Background

If you choose to make this background (it's entirely optional), you must do so before assembling the bouquet. First, review the weaving instructions on page 14. Then slip a sheet of graph paper under the plastic cover on your quilling board.

To form the center section, weave together twenty-seven horizontal lengths and twenty-one vertical lengths of ¼-inch-wide soft ivory paper.

To form each vertical border, add three lengths of ⅛-inch wide paper: teal, soft ivory, and teal—in that order.

To form each of the horizontal borders, first add a ⅛-wide teal strip, weaving it in the same pattern as the ¼-inch-wide soft ivory strip just beneath or above it rather than alternating the weaving direction as you would normally. (The teal and soft ivory strips should follow the same under/over pattern.) Next, add a ⅛-inch wide soft ivory and a ⅛-inch-wide teal strip, weaving them with the vertical strips as usual. Then add teal, soft ivory, and teal strips to each vertical border, weaving them as shown in the photo so that the teal in each corner is divided into four small squares. (You'll need to carry some soft ivory strips over two or more strips in order to do this.)

Add three more horizontal and three more vertical ¼-inch-wide soft ivory strips to complete the weaving. When you're finished, glue the weaving to a soft ivory mat board.

Assembly

Set aside the center bunny ear flower and the left-hand teardrop flower. Then, using the illustration as a guide, arrange the remaining flowers and greenery on the woven background and glue in place. Position the center bunny ear flower with its tip overlapping the upper teardrop flower and glue it in place. Position and glue the last teardrop flower on top of the bouquet. Using the photo as a guide, position the last leaf at an upward angle on the stem of the center teardrop flower and glue it in place. Arrange and glue the stems as shown in the illustration and trim their ends as necessary, cutting each one at an angle. Glue the bow on top of the gathered stems.

Gift Tag

Using the teardrop flower pattern on the previous page, make one light blue and turquoise teardrop flower. Roll two celadon green 1½-inch loose scrolls and two celadon green 2½-inch loose scrolls. Using the photo as a guide, glue each small scroll to a large scroll; then glue the paired scrolls to the flower. Cut a 3-inch by 5-inch card from soft ivory cover-weight paper, score the card across its length, and fold it in half. Glue the flower to the front of the card.

Fall Harvest Design

What better symbol of nature's bounty than a stunning collection of quilled fruit, straight from the autumn garden and orchard?

Tip

⯈ Use narrow paper unless another width is specified.

Pumpkin

To make the stem, roll four tan 3-inch marquises and three tan 3-inch triangles. Using the pattern as a guide, glue them together. Then pin the stem to the pattern, tilting it at an upward angle.

Fill in the pumpkin pattern with orange 4-inch marquises, gluing the shapes together as you work. Note that several of these shapes should be glued behind the angled stem.

Pumpkin Leaves *(make two)*

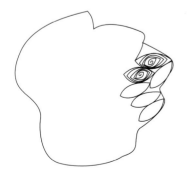

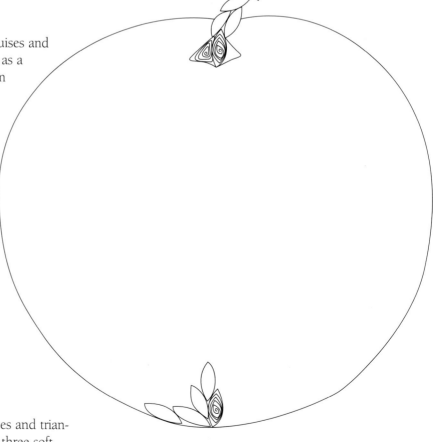

Fill in the pattern with green 3-inch marquises and triangles, gluing them together as you work. Roll three soft green loose spirals to serve as tendrils.

Apple

Fill in the pattern with red 3-inch marquises and crescents, gluing the shapes together as you work. Make the stem by rolling a short spiral, using ⅛-inch-wide brown paper, and glue it in place.

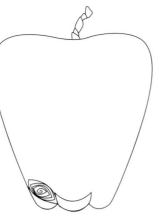

Pears

(make two)

To make each pear, fill in the pattern with bright yellow 3-inch marquises, gluing the shapes together. For the stem, roll a short spiral, using ⅛-inch-wide brown paper, and glue it in place.

Persimmons

(make three)

To make each persimmon, fill in the pattern with apricot 2-inch marquises, gluing them together. To make each calyx, roll five green 2-inch marquises and glue them on top of the fruit. Roll a short green spiral for the stem and glue it in place as well.

Wheat *(make four)*

For each wheat stalk, roll approximately fifteen tan 3-inch marquises. On the back of each one, glue a short pointed length of tan paper at one end. Then, using the illustration as a guide, glue the shapes together in two layers. Roll a spiral from ⅛-inch-wide tan paper and glue it in place as a stem.

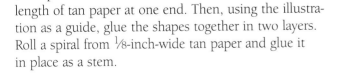

Grape Bunches *(make two)*

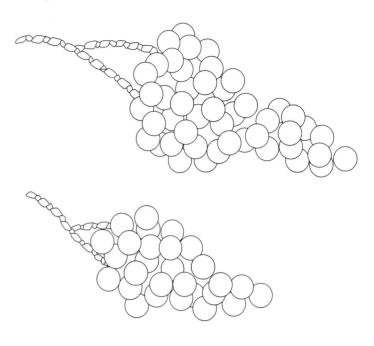

Fill in each pattern with three layers of purple 3-inch loose circles. For the stems, roll spirals from ⅛-inch-wide brown paper and glue them in place.

Assembly

Before assembling the design, shape and round the pumpkin, leaves, apple, pears, and persimmons. To do this, place a quilled piece in the palm of one hand with its front surface facing down. Then use the fingers of your other hand to press it gently until it's slightly concave.

Using the photo as a guide, position the pumpkin and leaves on the background and glue them in place. Add the three tendrils. Then arrange the rest of the fruit and the wheat and glue them in place.

Quilled Border

*This beautiful quilled border, with its graceful shapes and contours,
will lend a loving touch to any photograph or picture it surrounds..*

Tips

- Use 1/8-inch-wide paper unless another width is specified.
- To fringe 1/8-inch-wide paper, you must use scissors,
  as a fringing tool won't work with paper this narrow.
- The frame for this project is 6 inches by 8 inches, and
  the opening in the oval mat is $3\frac{1}{4}$ inches by 5 inches.

#1 Flowers (*make three*)

Make the petals for each flower by rolling and gluing together six aqua 5-inch marquises as shown in the pattern. For the flower center, roll a soft yellow 3-inch tight circle and glue it on top of the petals. To one flower, add three teal 2-inch loose scrolls and two teal 2½-inch loose scrolls as shown. To the other two flowers, add two teal 2-inch loose scrolls and one teal 2½-inch loose scroll.

#2 Flowers (*make four*)

For each flower, use the pattern to glue together five aqua 3-inch teardrops. Roll a soft yellow 1½-inch loose circle and glue it on top of the petals to serve as the flower's center. To make leaves, roll five seafoam green 2½-inch marquises. Add one each to three of the flowers and two to the remaining flower.

#3 Flowers (*make five*)

To make each flower, use the pattern for the #2 flowers to glue together five pink 3-inch teardrops. To make the flower center, roll a deep rose 2-inch tight circle and glue it in place. To make leaves, roll seven seafoam green 3-inch marquises. Also roll five seafoam green 2-inch loose scrolls. Glue one leaf and one loose scroll to each of three flowers. Glue two leaves and one loose scroll to each of the two remaining flowers.

#4 Flowers (*make ten*)

For each flower, use the pattern to glue four lavender 3-inch bunny ears together. To make the flower center, glue one end of a 1½-inch lavender length to one end of a 1½-inch purple length. Roll this long strip into a tight circle, beginning with the lavender end, and glue it on top of the petals.

To make the leaves, roll thirteen seafoam green 2½-inch teardrops. Add one leaf to each of five flowers and two leaves to each of four flowers. The remaining flower doesn't have any leaves.

Fringed Flower Sprays (*make six*)

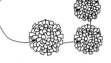

Make three fringed flowers for each spray, using 2-inch, 2½-inch, and 3-inch lengths of soft yellow paper. To make the stem, curve a short length of narrow seafoam green paper. Arrange the fringed flowers, positioning the smallest one at the stem's tip, and glue them in place.

Assembly

Using the illustration as a guide, position and glue the #1 flowers onto the mat first. Then add the #2, #3, and #4 flowers. Position and glue the six fringed flower sprays last.

Flared Border with Huskings

Made with huskings and unusual flared-paper shapes, this quilled border is a perfect complement to the treasured, sepia-toned photograph of the artist's family. Her father (at left), who was four years old when this photo was taken, is shown with two brothers and a sister.

Tips

‣ Use ⅛-inch-wide paper throughout.

‣ The artist who created this border gilds her own quilling paper. For a similar look, you may use special gilded paper, available through quilling suppliers. Alternatively, just select paper and background colors to complement your own photo and frame.

Flared Shapes for Border

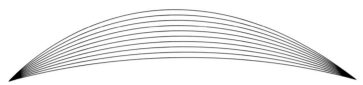

First measure the circumference of the oval (in this project, it's 30 inches) and divide that measurement by the number of flared shapes you want to make. (This designer thought that eight flared shapes would look well with her rather large frame.) The result, 3¾ inches for this oval, will be the length of each flared shape where it meets the oval border.

To make each flared section, cut ten lengths of paper, each about 1 inch longer than the measurement you calculated and stack them on top of one another. (Cutting these straight from a package of quilling strips is easiest.) Hold the stack by its ends and bend it into a horseshoe shape while letting the ends slip slightly through your fingers. Then grip the ends tightly and straighten the stack out again. The upper strips in the stack should flare upward by about ½ inch. Trim the ends as necessary to even them out and glue them together securely.

Long Double Curls (*make twenty-four*)

Cut a 3½-inch length of paper and fold it ¼ inch off center. Curl the folded end slightly. To open the doubled paper within the curl, pull the shorter end even with the longer end; then glue the ends together.

Short Double Curls (*make twenty-four*)

Following the instructions for making long double curls, use 2½-inch lengths of paper to make these shorter double curls.

Small Huskings (*make twenty-four*)

First, review the instructions for making huskings on page 13. Then make these small huskings, using the pin-placement pattern provided here. Wrap each husking three times before gluing the end of the paper down.

Large Huskings (*make twelve*)

Repeat to make the large huskings, using the pin-placement pattern provided.

Large Grape Rolls (*make eight*)

Roll a 12-inch length of paper into a grape roll.

Small Grape Rolls (*make forty*)

Roll a 6-inch length of paper into a grape roll.

Assembly

Position the eight flared shapes around the edge of the oval in the mat board and glue them in place. Using the photo as a guide, glue three small grape rolls at the top of each flared shape.

Using the illustration and photo as guides, at each point where the flared shapes meet, arrange and glue two large double curls, two small double curls, and three small huskings. Glue a large grape roll on top, as shown.

To create each of the flowers in the frame corners, first refer to the illustration above. Then glue together three large huskings, two large double curls, and two small double curls. Add a large grape roll to serve as the flower's center and glue the flower to the background. Glue together a group of three small grape rolls, position as shown, and glue in place.

Gloriosa (or Flame) Lily

Brilliant petal colors, slender stems, and delicate stamens characterize this beautiful gathering of quilled flame lilies

Tips

❧ Use ⅛-inch-wide paper unless another width is specified.

❧ Remove each lily, leaf, or bud from your quilling work board after gluing it together so that you have room to work on the next shape.

Large Lily

Begin by reviewing the looping instructions on page 12. Then, using the pattern provided, make four looped petals, starting each one with three gold loops, continuing with three red loops, and adding a larger yellow loop around the outside.

Roll the tip of each outermost yellow loop as shown. Then, using a slotted needle tool, crease the two outermost loops of each petal at various locations.

Using the pattern provided, repeat to make two smaller petals, each with three gold loops, two red loops, and one yellow loop. Crease these as before.

Gently curve the six petals as shown in the illustration on the opposite page. Using this pattern as a guide, glue the four large petals together and add the two smaller ones of top of them. Add a dark green 6-inch length to serve as a stem. Make a lime green 6-inch triangle and glue a lime green 2-inch loose scroll to its base. Then glue the triangle to the bottom of the lily.

To make the six stamens, roll six gold 1-inch loose circles and glue each one to a narrow 1-inch length of dark green paper. Glue three stamens to each side of the lily.

Small Lily *(left)*

Create three more small looped petals, but make two of these with gold rather than yellow outer loops. Using the assembly pattern, shape and glue the three petals together. Make a dark green 2½-inch triangle, glue a dark green 2-inch loose scroll to its base, and glue the triangle to the bottom of the small lily. Add a dark green 5-inch length as a stem. Make three more stamens and glue these in place as well.

Small Lily *(right)*

Make this lily as you did the other small lily, but loop all three petals with gold, red, and yellow loops. Add a lime green triangle and loose scroll, a dark green 5-inch stem, and six stamens.

Bud

The bud (at the upper left of the assembly pattern) consists of two looped shapes, each started with four yellow loops and finished with two lime green loops. Use a slotted quilling tool to crease the inner edge of each looped shape, as shown in the pattern. Then glue the two shapes together. Add a dark green 3½-inch stem, gluing it to the top of the bud.

Leaves (*make four*)

The four leaves are made with a total of eight 6-inch teardrops (five dark green and three lime green) and eight 4-inch marquises (five dark green and three lime green). Using the pattern provided and the photo as a color guide, glue these shapes together in sets of four.

Next, using the instructions that follow, wrap one leaf in a 7-inch length of lime green and three leaves in 7-inch lengths of dark green. Glue one end of the long strip to the bottom of a leaf, between the teardrops, and continue by gluing it almost up to the leaf tip. Repeat with the other end of the long strip. You'll be left with a large loop above the leaf itself. Fold and roll down this loop as shown. Add a 1-inch-long dark green stem to one of the leaves and a 1½-inch-long stem to another.

Assembly

Position the flowers and buds on the assembly pattern and glue the stems together where the pattern shows them touching each other. Add the two leaves with stems, gluing the stems as shown. Then carefully glue the entire piece to the background, leaving the stamens and triangle shapes free. Position and glue the remaining two leaves on top of the flower stems.

Teddy Bear

*Light-hearted subjects are just as suitable for quilling as more serious designs.
This whimsical teddy, waving from behind his garden wall, will greet you warmly
no matter where you display him.*

Tips

- Use narrow paper unless another width is specified.
- You'll need some tissue paper for this project, in dark green, dark brown, and olive green. Also make sure you have a few cocktail sticks on hand.
- Parts of this design were made with very narrow (1/32-inch) strips of quilling paper. You may either make these by cutting narrow (1/16-inch) strips in half along their lengths or use 1/16-inch-wide strips instead.

Gate Sticks *(make sixteen)*

To make each of the gate sticks (fourteen vertical and two horizontal), roll a 1½-inch square of dark green tissue paper diagonally around a cocktail stick. Secure the corner of the tissue paper with glue and remove the cocktail stick.

Trim fourteen of these paper rolls to 1⅝ inches in length. Using the illustration as a guide, glue these onto the background.

Glue a length of green quilling paper along the bottom edge of the glued sticks. Position the remaining two sticks horizontally across the gate, trim them to length, and glue them in place.

Gate Sides *(make two)*

Roll two more sticks, using 1½-inch squares, as before, but add two more squares of dark green tissue paper to each one in order to make them thicker. Trim the paper rolls to just under 1¾ inches in length. Roll two 3-inch tight circles from very narrow dark green quilling paper and glue one flat on top of one end of each stick. Glue the sticks to the outer edges of the gate.

Gateposts *(make two)*

To make each post, first roll a 1½-inch square of dark brown tissue paper around a cocktail stick as before; then add three more squares to each stick for extra thickness.

Remove the cocktail stick and trim to 1¾ inches in length. Using very narrow dark brown paper, roll two 3-inch tight circles and glue them flat on top of the posts. Roll two 3-inch grape rolls from very narrow dark brown paper and glue them, on edge, to the tops of the tight circles on the posts. Then glue the gate posts in place.

Brick Wall

Roll a series of 4-inch rectangles and 2¼-inch squares, using lengths of brown, tan, beige, and gray quilling paper. Begin constructing the wall at its base, leaving a small gap between each of the nine rows. When you're finished, glue a length of tan quilling paper along the top edge of each wall portion and add a length made of finely crimped tan paper to each one as well.

Tip

‣ Assemble all flowers and leaves before gluing them to the background.

Tall Flowers (make five)

Choose shades of scarlet, tangerine, and yellow for these flowers. Using the pattern as a guide, make fifteen 1½-inch narrow oval shapes and forty 2¼-inch narrow oval shapes. (These will serve to make all five flowers.) Make a sturdy stem for each flower by gluing two lengths of green quilling paper together. Using the pattern as a guide, glue the oval shapes to the stems, placing three smaller ovals at the top of each one.

Make a total of sixteen shaped teardrop leaves, using 3-inch green paper lengths, and add them to the flowers. Also make a 3-inch peg for each flower and glue it to the back of each flower stalk, at the top.

Sunflower

To make the center, roll a duo-tone fringed flower using 9-inch lengths of ³⁄₁₆-inch-wide paper in two shades of brown. Using the looping method, make thirty yellow double-loop petals next; each one should be ⅜-inch from top to bottom. Glue the petals together in six sets of five. Then glue the sets around the fringed flower center.

Make the stem by rolling a 2-inch square of olive green tissue paper diagonally around a thin wire. Remove the wire and trim the roll to 2 inches in length. Glue this stem to the sunflower head, between any two petals.

Using the looping method, make five green sunflower leaves and edge each one with a single length of paper. Glue the leaves to the sunflower stem. Roll a 3-inch tight circle and glue it to the back of the flower as a peg.

Red Flowers *(make five)*

For each flower, glue together four red 1½-inch rolled hearts. To make the flower center, roll a ¾-inch tight circle, using very narrow black paper, and glue it to the center of the flower.

White Daisies *(make six)*

For each daisy, make six teardrops, using 1½-inch lengths of very narrow white paper. Glue the petals together and, as a flower center, add a ¾-inch tight circle made with very narrow gold paper.

Orange Daisies *(make six)*

Select three shades of very narrow orange paper and make two flowers in each shade. For each flower, make six 1½-inch teardrops and glue them together. To make a center for each daisy, roll a ¾-inch tight circle, using very narrow brown paper.

Fringed Flowers *(make five orange and five cream)*

Using scissors, fringe ten 3-inch lengths of ⅛-inch-wide paper. Roll each length to make a fringed flower.

Leaves

Using very narrow paper, roll a total of forty-three marquises: twenty-two made with 1½-inch green lengths; thirteen made with 2-inch light green lengths; and eight made with 2-inch dark green lengths.

Assembly

Using the pattern and photo as guides and starting at the base, glue all the flowers and leaves to the brick wall.

Earth

Roll approximately seventy 1½-inch loose circles, using 1-inch lengths of very narrow brown paper. Glue these beneath the brick wall, as shown in the photo.

Teddy Bear

Cut the teddy-bear pattern from thin card stock. Make approximately seventy 2¼-inch fringed flowers from ¼-inch-wide tan paper. Fill in the pattern completely, gluing the flowers together to resemble fur.

To form a snout, glue three of these flowers on top of the others. For the nose, make a 1¼-inch rolled heart from very narrow black paper. For the eyes, roll two 1½-inch tight circles from very narrow black paper. Glue the nose and eyes in place. To make the mouth, use short lengths of very narrow black paper, gluing them on edge.

To make the neck ribbon, roll a spiral with very narrow red paper, trim it to fit, and glue it in place. Roll two 2¼-inch rolled hearts with very narrow red paper and glue them to the ribbon. Then glue the teddy bear to the background.

Spray of Flowers

Nature's simplest designs sometimes offer the most exquisite visual pleasures. This quilled flower spray is an excellent example.

Tips

- The oval opening in the 6-inch by 8-inch frame shown in the photo is 4½ inches by 6½ inches.
- Paper widths are specified in the instructions.

Border

Using narrow cadet blue paper, roll long spirals to make a border for your frame opening. You'll need more than one spiral; just glue them together end to end.

Large Fringed Flowers *(make nine)*

Using 8-inch lengths of ⅜-inch-wide paper, make five cadet blue and four pale peach fringed flowers.

Medium Fringed Flowers *(make six)*

Using 3-inch lengths of ⅜-inch-wide paper, make three cadet blue and three pale peach fringed flowers. Spread the fringes only part of the way open. To make a calyx for each flower, roll a 4¼-inch grape roll, using green ⅛-inch-wide paper. Glue a flower into each calyx.

Buds *(make eight)*

Using 1½-inch lengths of fringed ¼-inch-wide paper, roll six pale peach and two cadet blue buds. To make a calyx for each one, roll a 3-inch grape roll, using green ⅛-inch-wide paper. Glue a bud into each calyx.

Leaves *(make fourteen)*

Roll a green 4-inch marquise, using ⅛-inch-wide paper.

Assembly

Glue the spiral border to the background, just inside the frame opening. Using the photo as a guide, make stems by cutting and shaping three lengths of green ⅛-inch-wide paper. Arrange the stems and glue them to the background. Position and glue the flowers, buds, and leaves.

Swans

Consider making this beautiful quilled project as a gift for a loved one. The gracefully arched necks of the lovely swans send a very special message.

Tips

‣ Use narrow paper unless another width is specified.

‣ The oval mat opening shown in the photo is 5¼ inches by 6 inches.

‣ A ¹⁄₁₆-inch hole punch and a punch that makes small heart shapes will come in handy when you make the flower bunches for this project. Both tools are available from quilling suppliers. You can always cut these shapes by hand, of course, but doing so will take time and patience!

‣ Make two tracings of the swan-neck and body patterns before you start.

Swan Necks *(make two)*

Each neck is made by braiding two strips of paper together. Although this technique is easy once you get the hang of it, you'll probably want to practice first.

Glue four full lengths of white paper together at their ends to form a cross with four "legs." To help you keep track of which leg is which, attach a small piece of tape to the end of each one and, using the illustration as a guide, label the tags with the numbers 1, 2, 3, and 4.

Fold leg #1 down between #2 and #3.

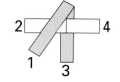

Fold leg #2 across #1 and #3 so that it rests between #3 and #4.

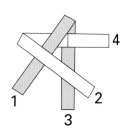

Fold leg #3 up across #2 and #4.

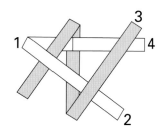

This step is slightly tricky. Carefully bring leg #4 over #3, but before you crease it, weave it under leg #1. Then gently pull the legs so that their edges touch.

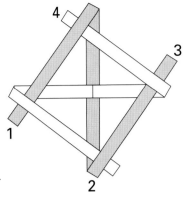

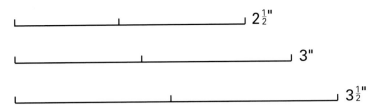

Now turn the braid around so that leg #1 is at the top again and repeat the previous braiding steps in sequence, moving leg #1 between #2 and #3, and so on, until the braided neck is 4 inches long. To finish off, glue each strip at the top and trim away the excess paper.

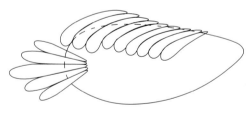

Place the traced neck patterns on your work board, flipping one over to reverse it. (The two necks will form a heart shape when they're placed side by side.) To shape the necks, carefully bend them to fit these patterns and pin them in place onto the patterns while you work on other portions of the project.

To make the eyes, glue either a small black bead or a small black paper cutout to each neck. For the beaks, cut out black paper beak shapes and glue them in place.

Swan Bodies (make two)

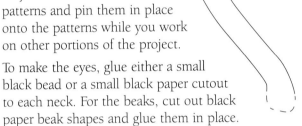

To make one body, fill in one tracing of the body pattern (omitting the tail and wing feathers) with bright white 2-inch marquises. Flip the other body tracing over and use it to make the other swan body.

Wings and Tail Feathers (make two of each)

Use the traced patterns, one flipped over to reverse it, as you carry out the following instructions.

Each wing is made up of nine bright white looped shapes: six made with 3-inch lengths and three made with 3½-inch lengths. To make each shape, fold the paper length ¼-inch off center. (The folding points are marked in the illustrations above.) Form a loop with the shorter section and glue the end to the fold. Loop the longer section around this small loop and glue the end in place. Flatten each looped shape slightly to match the shapes in the wing portion of the swan pattern; then glue the shapes together to form the wing.

Each set of tail feathers is also made up of bright white looped shapes: one 3½-inch shape in the center, two 3-inch shapes on either side of it, and a 2½-inch shape on each outer edge. Make these loops as before and use the tail-feather portion of the swan pattern to glue them together.

Flowers (make four)

Take a look at the four flower bunches in the photo. To make the backgrounds for these bunches, use the photo as a guide to cut four small shapes from any type of paper. Next, cut or punch out a batch of circles and a separate batch of small hearts from ⅜-inch-wide cadet blue paper. Spread glue onto one of the four paper patterns and cover it with a layer of cutout circles, overlapping the circles slightly. Then add a layer of overlapping cutout hearts, gluing each one in place. Punch or cut out four hearts from green ⅜-inch-wide paper and glue them to the top of each bunch. Repeat to make the other three flower bunches.

Assembly

Using the photo as a guide, position the necks on the background to form a slightly open heart and glue them in place. Glue the wings and tail feathers to the bodies; then glue the bodies to the background with their front ends overlapping the bottoms of the necks.

Roll small loose scrolls at both ends of two 2½-inch lengths of green paper; then glue two flower bunches to the center edge of each length. Position the two sets of flowers with their green ends and scrolls above the oval opening in the mat.

Quilt-Block Designs

Geometric quilt-block designs, as these beautiful projects prove, lend themselves perfectly to quilling. They'll also provide you with plenty of practice making identical shapes.

Broken Star

Tips

- Use 3-inch lengths of ⅛-inch-wide paper throughout.
- To help guarantee matched diamond shapes, use the smallest molds in a quilling/designer board when you make the loose circles.

This entire design is made with 3-inch diamonds. You may use any colors you like, but a combination of light, medium, and dark shades will look best. If you like the colors shown in the photo, use teal (A), mauve (B), and soft ivory (C).

Make ninety-six teal diamonds, ninety-six mauve diamonds, and ninety-six soft ivory diamonds.

Assembly

Using the pattern provided and starting with the shapes in the center of the design, glue the pieces together. Then glue the assembled quilt block onto your background.

40

Rose of Sharon

Tip

‣ Use ⅛-inch-wide paper unless another width is specified.

Flower

For the lower layer, roll eight pale dusty rose 4-inch teardrops. For the upper layer, use narrow soft ivory paper to roll eight 2½-inch teardrops. Glue together the petals for each flower; then glue the smaller flower on top of the larger one as shown. Add a pale dusty rose 2-inch tight circle, made with narrow paper, as a flower center.

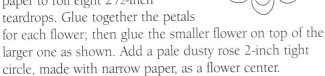

Buds, Calyxes, and Stems

(make four of each)

Roll a pale dusty rose 3-inch marquise and a celadon green 3-inch bunny ear, taking care to shape the bunny ear quite tightly. Glue the bud into the calyx as shown. For stems, set aside two ½-inch and two ¾-inch lengths of celadon green paper.

Leaves *(make forty-four)*

Roll a celadon green 2-inch marquise.

Assembly

Glue the leaves to the stems. Glue the flower to the background first. Then add the stems with leaves, positioning them so that they're symmetrical. Add the buds with calyxes last.

Prairie Flower

Tip

➤ Use ⅛-inch-wide paper unless another width is specified.

Flower

Roll eight pale dusty rose 4-inch teardrops for the lower layer. For the upper layer, roll five 3-inch bunny ears, using narrow soft ivory paper. Glue together the petals of each flower; then glue the bunny ear flower on top of the teardrop flower. Cut a narrow 2-inch length of pale dusty rose paper in half along its length. Then use one of these very narrow strips to roll a loose circle and add it as a flower center.

Buds with Calyxes and Stems

(make three)

Roll a pale dusty rose 2-inch marquise for each bud. For the calyxes, roll six celadon green 1⅛-inch crescents and glue two crescents to each bud as shown. Set aside one ⅜-inch and one 2¾-inch length of celadon green paper to use as stems.

Leaves *(make twenty-three)*

Roll nineteen 2-inch marquises and four 1½-inch marquises.

Assembly

Glue two of the larger leaves and a bud with calyxes to the short stem. Then glue this short stem to the flower.

Glue a bud with calyx to one end of each of the longer stems and add two of the smaller leaves at the top of each stem as well. Then add the remaining large leaves to the stems as shown. Using the photo as a guide, position the long curved stem and the flower with short stem on the background and glue them in place.

Tiger Cub

This adorable tiger cub, frolicking in the grass, will bring a smile to your face every time you catch a glimpse of him.

Tips

- Use ⅛-inch-wide paper unless another width is specified.

- The oval frame opening shown in the photo is 7½ inches by 9½ inches.

- After gluing together the shapes that make up one part of the tiger, remove that assembly from the tiger pattern so that you can see the outlines of the next part you need to make. If you leave the head in place, for example, you won't be able to see the full neck outline.

Tiger Ears
(make two)

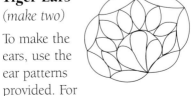

To make the ears, use the ear patterns provided. For each ear, first glue together three orange 3-inch teardrops. Then wrap the glued teardrops with a length of black paper. Roll eight orange 2-inch marquises and glue them around the teardrops. Roll seven orange 4-inch marquises and glue them in place as well.

Head

Roll three black 4-inch teardrops and six black 3-inch teardrops. Using the head portion of the tiger pattern (see page 44), place one 4-inch and two 3-inch teardrops at the top of the head, with the 4-inch shape in the center. Position one 4-inch and two 3-inch teardrops on each side of the head, with the 4-inch shape at the top.

Glue a 24-inch length and a 12-inch length of black paper together, end to end. Roll a rounded grape roll with this 36-inch length to serve as the tiger's nose.

To make the long mouth sections, first double two lengths of black paper. Then curve each doubled length to match the pattern, glue it closed, and trim the ends to size. Make the short black lengths at the ends of the mouth with two doubled ½-inch lengths of black paper. Using the pattern, glue the four lengths together.

To make the eyes, roll two 24-inch lengths of light green paper into slightly loose tight circles and pinch each one into a marquise. Roll two 2-inch tight circles, using narrow black paper, and glue one to the center of each eye.

Position the nose, mouth, and eyes on the pattern and fill in the rest of the head area with orange 3-inch marquises.

Body and Tail

Roll eleven black 4-inch marquises. Arrange and glue them, as shown in the pattern, to form the three stripes on the tiger's back. Roll six black 5-inch teardrops and position these on the tail portion of the pattern.

Fill in the rest of the body area with orange 4-inch marquises and the rest of the tail area with orange 3-inch marquises. Then add a black 5-inch crescent to form the rounded tip of the tail.

Legs (total of four)

To make the toes, roll twelve orange 3-inch teardrops and outline each one with a length of black paper.

For the leg stripes, roll eight black 4-inch triangles and three black 2-inch triangles. The 2-inch triangles will go on the tiger's right front leg and the 4-inch triangles will go on the left front and rear legs.

Assemble the legs one at a time, using the patterns provided and filling in the sections around the toes and stripes with orange 3-inch marquises.

Tufts of Grass (make two)

Using the photo as a guide, glue together three single loops made with short lengths of green paper.

Assembly

Glue the ears to the back of the head. Make a 12-inch orange tight circle and glue it to the back of the head as a peg, between the eyes. Glue the head onto the body so that it overlaps the neck. Glue the left front and left rear legs to the front of the body, and the right front and right rear legs to its back. Then glue the tiger to the background. Position the tufts of grass and glue them in place as well.

Candles *(make three)*

Place an 8-inch square of red paper flat on your work surface and glue a length of orange or peach paper along each of two adjoining edges. Trim away the excess lengths.

Flip the square over and, beginning at the corner without added paper lengths, roll the square into a tight tube and glue down the corner. Then, using very sharp scissors, cut the tube in half to make two candles. Repeat with another piece of red paper.

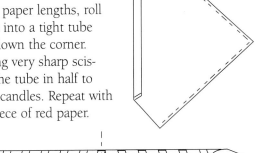

When you're finished, select the three best candles. If you like, you can trim their bottom ends to vary the heights.

Candle Wicks *(make three)*

For each wick, roll a ³/₄-inch square of brown or black paper, just as you rolled the candles. Glue one wick to the top of each candle.

Candle Flames *(make three)*

The three flames, made with the looping method, are 2 inches, 1¹/₂ inches, and 2 inches in height. Start each flame with three red loops; add three yellow loops to the smallest flame, four yellow loops to the medium flame, and five yellow loops to the largest flame. Remember to glue each loop at the bottom as you work.

Shape the finished flames as shown in the photo. Rest the candles flat on the table, glue each flame to a candle wick, and allow the glue to dry before attempting to stand the candles upright.

Candle Bases *(make three)*

To stabilize each candle, you must make a base for it. Start by cutting fringes on an 18-inch length of ³/₄-inch-wide green paper, leaving a ¹/₈-inch-wide area uncut along one edge. Glue one end of this fringed length to the bottom of a candle, with the fringes facing the flame. Roll the length tightly around the candle and glue down its end. Spread out the fringes as far as

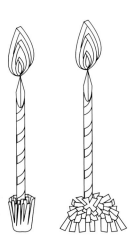

Christmas Centerpiece

Tired of Christmas candles that have to be lit every time you want to enjoy them? Try these cheerful tapers instead. Santa will love them, and so will your family on Christmas day.

Tips

- Use ¹/₈-inch-wide paper unless another width is specified.
- An oval or circle of wood, cork, or mat board, 6 to 8 inches across, makes a good base for this project.
- Treating the finished centerpiece with spray varnish will protect the paper.

45

possible so that the outer ones will touch the base when the candle is standing.

Fir Cones (*make four*)

Fringe an 18-inch length of ¾-inch-wide brown paper, making the cuts about ⅛-inch apart. Using the illustrations as guides, roll a tight circle with this length, glue down the end, and spread the fringes. Then gently push the point of a pencil up into the center to form a cone shape. To prevent the cone from collapsing, coat its inner surface with glue.

Greenery (*make seven*)

Loop a length of bright green paper as shown in the illustrations above. Vary the sizes of the pieces of greenery by adding more loops to some and by making some loops larger than others.

Assembly

Cut a decorative piece of red paper and glue it in the center of the base. Arrange and glue the three candles in the center, with a fir cone among them. Using the photo as a guide, glue the flowers in place. Add the remaining fir cones and the larger pieces of greenery. Then add the smaller pieces of greenery. Finally, add the berries in groups of two or three.

Berries (*make eight*)

Position a 9-inch length of ¼-inch wide red paper on your work surface and cut it diagonally along its length. (Each cut section will make one berry.) Starting at the wide end, roll one cut length tightly and glue down its point.

Christmas Roses (*make three*)

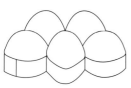

To make each petal, you'll need six or seven 18-inch lengths of bright white paper. Roll one length into a tight circle, add the next length and roll it, and continue until the circle is ½ inch in diameter. Shape the tight circle into a grape roll; then pinch the grape roll to shape the petal. Coat the outer surface with glue.

To assemble each flower, place five petals upside down and glue them together as shown. To make a center for each flower, roll seven yellow 1-inch loose circles and glue them together. Glue one set to each flower where the cupped petals meet.

Earrings and Brooch

Quilled jewelry can be as daring or discreet, as playful or elegant as you like. Once you've made the stunning examples shown here, you'll be more than ready to fill your jewelry box with designs of your own.

Tips

- Use either ⅛-inch-wide or narrow paper throughout. (Narrow paper will lend a more delicate look to your jewelry.)

- Select any paper colors you like. Gold quill trim can look wonderful, and jewelry touched up with a special gilding pen is also lovely. To add a special touch to any husking, use two different colors: one for the wraps around the pins and another for the final wraps around the entire husking.

- To vary the shapes and sizes of huskings, move the pins closer together or farther apart or add an extra pair of pins.

- Jewelry findings (small items such as jump rings, earring hooks, and brooch pins) are available from many jewelry stores and bead shops. A jump ring is a small metal ring with a slit in it. You'll join each earring to a hook by looping a jump ring through both and pressing the ring closed with small pliers.

- Waterproofing your jewelry is easy. Before adding the findings, place the jewelry on a sheet of aluminum foil and apply two coats of spray varnish or clear nail polish. (Let the first coat dry thoroughly before applying the second.)

Making Huskings

Review the instructions on page 13 before you begin. The huskings for these projects are made with 24-inch lengths of paper that have been folded in half.

Trace the pin-placement patterns and slip the one you need (small or medium) behind the plastic on your quilling work board. Insert the pins and start each husking by looping the center fold over pin #1. Then wind the doubled paper around the other pins as shown in the illustrations at the bottom of this page.

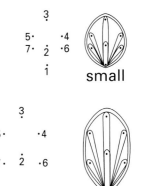

Making Open Circles

These shapes are simply tight circles with large holes in their centers. They're made by rolling a length of paper several times around a cylindrical object thicker than a quilling tool. (Fat toothpicks and thin dowels work well.) To graduate the circle sizes, use short lengths of paper for smaller circles and longer lengths for larger circles.

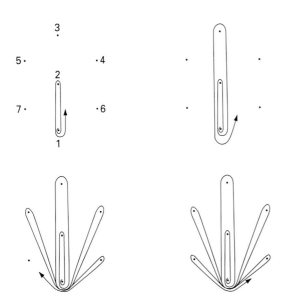

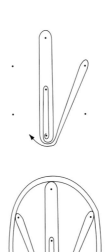

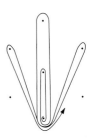

Single Drop Earrings

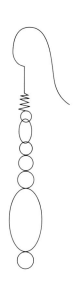

Make two medium huskings and eight open circles (four large, two medium, and two small). To assemble each earring, first glue one small, one medium, and one large open circle together in a row. Then glue the large open circle in this row to the top of a husking. Add another large open circle to the bottom of the husking. Join the small open circle and earring hook with a jump ring. (For added length, include another jump ring between the first jump ring and the hook.)

Three-Drop Earrings

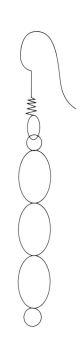

Make six small huskings and four open circles (two medium and two large). Assemble each earring as shown, with the large open circle at the bottom.

Graduated Two-Drop Earrings

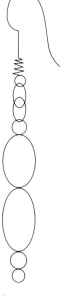

Make two small huskings, two medium huskings, and six open circles (two large, two medium, and two small). Using the illustration as a guide, glue two huskings together for each earring. Add a medium open circle at the top of each earring and a large and small open circle at the bottom. Attach one or two jump rings and a hook to each earring.

Miniature Frame Earrings

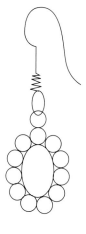

Make two small huskings and twenty-two to twenty-four small open circles. To make sure the circles are identical, roll them using the same tool and paper strips of equal length. Assemble as shown.

Flower Earrings

Make ten small huskings and fourteen medium open circles. Assemble as shown.

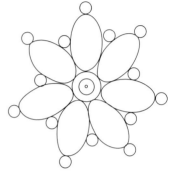

Flower Brooch

Make seven small huskings and fourteen 3-inch tight circles. Take two 9-inch lengths of paper, each a different color, and glue them together end to end. Then roll the 18-inch length into a tight circle.

Glue the huskings around the large tight circle and add the small tight circles as shown. Varnish, if desired, before using a very strong glue to affix a brooch pin to the back.

Hudson Model 20
(1910)

Here's the perfect gift for someone addicted to antique cars! This miniature paper replica of a classic Hudson looks real enough to roll right off the page.

Tips

- Use ⅛-inch-wide paper unless another width is specified.
- You'll need a 1-inch-diameter dowel in order to wind the wheels.
- Make the various sections of the car before assembling them on the background.

Car Body *(below fenders and running board)*

Fill in these two portions of the pattern with black 1-inch tight circles.

Fenders and Running Board

Cut three 6-inch lengths of ⅜-inch-wide red paper and glue them together, face to face, to make a single layered strip. Use the pattern to bend this strip to shape.

Car Body and Seat
(above fenders and running board)

As shown in the pattern, the upper car body and seat consist of four separate sections: A, B, C, and D. If you look at the photo, you'll see that these are separated from one another by layered strips of gold paper. Start by filling in the four upper car-body and seat pattern areas with red 1-inch tight circles. Set the four small assemblies aside when you're finished. Next, glue together three full lengths of gold paper, face to face. When you assemble the car, you'll cut lengths from this strip to serve as dividers. You'll also use this layered strip to make the roof framework and other parts.

Radiator and Headlight

To create the radiator, glue short strips of gold paper to the upper, front, and top front edges of car-body section D. Roll a ¾-inch tight circle, using narrow gold paper, and glue it to the top of the gold radiator. Cut a small gold shape to represent the headlight and set it aside.

Cab

The framework over which the two roof sections are glued consists of six "sticks." To make these, cut six lengths from your layered gold strip, using the cab-framework portion of the pattern to gauge their sizes. Glue the six pieces together as shown.

Cut the two roof sections from ⅜-inch-wide soft ivory paper and set them aside.

Steering Wheel and Gear Shift

To make the steering column, glue three very narrow lengths of black paper together, face to face. Use the pattern to trim this layered strip to length. Make a steering wheel by gluing three very narrow lengths of brown paper together, face to face, and trimming the layered strip to length.

To make the two gearshift sticks, first cut a short length from your layered gold strip. Then cut this short layered strip almost all the way down its length. Bend the two sections away from each other to create two sticks. To make handles, cut two very short lengths from your layered gold strip and glue one at the top of each stick.

Wheels *(make two)*

To make each wheel, first roll a 36-inch length of black paper tightly around a 1-inch-diameter dowel and glue its end down. Then roll white paper around the black paper

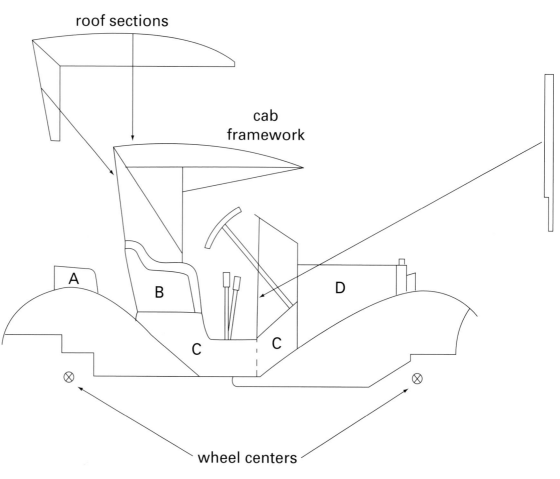

roof sections

cab framework

A B C C D

wheel centers

until the wheel's diameter is $1\frac{5}{16}$ inches. Glue the end of the white paper down securely.

Remove the wheel from the dowel and add the spokes by gluing six short lengths of narrow red paper across its back. To make the hub cap, roll a tight circle, using an 8-inch length of narrow black paper, and add a narrow gold $1\frac{1}{2}$-inch tight circle on top. Turn the wheel over so the spokes are on the back and glue the cap to the center of the spokes.

Assembly

You'll assemble the car on a piece of dark, heavyweight paper that matches the outline of the upper and lower car body and the seat. Then you'll glue the assembled car onto the background in your frame.

Cut the dark paper pattern piece first and glue the two black lower car-body sections to it. Then add the fenders and running board.

Using the photo as a guide, cut lengths from your layered gold strip to outline the red upper car-body sections and seat. (Note that the gold length between car-body sections C and D extends above the body itself. Don't cut the notched dashboard strip yet.) Glue these lengths to the edges of the car-body sections; then glue the car-body sections to the dark paper background.

Roll ten 2-inch tight circles, using narrow brown paper, and glue them to the gold paper on the top and front of the seat. Also glue the gold headlight to the background, just in front of the radiator.

Bend the layered brown steering-wheel into an arc shape and glue it to the top of the steering column. Next, using the pattern as a guide, glue the bottom of the steering wheel column to the center of the gold strip on the car floor. (The column shouldn't touch the background of your finished, framed piece.)

Now cut a length of the layered gold paper to serve as the dashboard, making a notch in its bottom, as shown in the illustration. Glue this piece in place, on edge, so that its narrow tail overlaps car-body section C. Cut another short length of layered gold for the angled windshield and, using the photo as a guide, glue it to the tops of the two vertical gold strips.

Glue the gear shift, on edge, to car-body section C. Then glue the cab framework to the brown tight circles on the seat. (The framework should not touch the background.) Glue the two roof sections to the framework as shown. Position the wheels and glue them to the black body sections. Finally, turn the assembled car over, apply glue to the heavyweight paper, and glue the car to the background.

Carolina Wren and Apple Blossoms

No wonder this tiny wren looks so happy. Winter has passed, warm spring breezes caress the trees, and the world is filled with delicate white apple blossoms.

Tips

- Use $\frac{1}{8}$-inch-wide paper unless another width is specified.
- The frame opening shown in the photo is $4\frac{1}{2}$ inches by $6\frac{1}{2}$ inches.

Beak

Fold an $\frac{11}{16}$-inch length of brown paper in half. Fold an $\frac{11}{16}$-inch length of gold paper in half. Insert the folded gold length into the folded brown length and glue the lengths together. Trim the layered paper into a beak shape and curve it slightly.

Bird

To make the eye, roll a black ½-inch tight circle and wrap a length of silver grey paper once around it. Position this roll on the pattern. Roll six white ½-inch tight circles and position them in a row above the eye. Roll six brown 1-inch marquises. Glue three above the white tight circles and three below the white circles and eye.

Fill in the throat area with twelve white ½-inch tight circles. Fill in the breast area with ivory ½-inch tight circles. Fill in the back and tail area with rust 1-inch teardrops, scattering seven or eight brown 1-inch teardrops through the tail.

Glue a length of rust paper along the edge of the bird, from the point where the bill meets the top of the head to the point where the tail meets the ivory breast. Glue a length of ivory to the edge of the breast and a length of white to the edge of the throat.

Glue two ½-inch lengths of narrow tan paper together face to face, curve one end to form a foot, and glue the foot to the bird's breast.

Apple Blossoms (make four)

For each blossom, roll five 12-inch tight circles, using narrow white paper. Let each circle loosen slightly and pinch a point on each one. Roll a soft green 1-inch tight circle. Using the photo and pattern as guides, glue the pointed ends of the petals to the tight circle, elevating the petals and angling and overlapping some as well. Cut two or three ¼-inch lengths of yellow paper, fringe one end of each, and roll the fringed ends. Glue these fringed strips to the edges of the soft green tight circle so that the fringes curve up and around its top.

Buds (make ten)

For each bud, roll three tight circles, using 12-inch lengths of narrow pink paper and letting each one loosen just a tiny bit before gluing it closed. Pinch one side to a point. Shape the pinched tight circles into very shallow grape rolls and spread glue on their concave surfaces. Using the photo as a guide, glue the three shapes together, two with their rounded surfaces up and one with the rounded surface down. Make a calyx for each bud by cutting two or three short, pointed shapes from green paper and gluing them to the base of the bud grouping.

Leaves (make fifteen)

For each leaf, roll a teardrop, using a 12-inch length of narrow green paper.

Limbs

Glue a grey 1-inch length and a brown 1½-inch length together end to end. Roll this strip into a rounded rectangle, beginning with the brown end. Repeat to make twenty-three rectangles. Then, using the pattern, glue these together to make the limbs. You'll need seventeen for the longest limb, five for the medium limb, and one for the very short limb behind the lowest apple blossom.

Assembly

Glue the limbs to the background. Position the flowers and buds and glue them in place. Add the leaves next. Roll two small pegs and glue them to the back of the bird, one to the tail and one to the body. Position the bird with the body and foot overlapping the limb and glue it in place.

A house is not a home without a guardian angel. Fortunately, inviting one to take up residence is easy. Create a host of these exquisite quilled versions, at least one for yourself and several for the homes of friends.

Tips

- For angels with medium complexions, use ⅛-inch-wide soft ivory paper unless another width or color is specified. For angels with dark complexions, use tan paper when making the head and hair.

- The instructions that follow mention "seams" quite frequently. The seam is the point on any shape where the end of the paper length is glued down.

- To help these angels achieve immortality, you must spray them with a clear acrylic spray sealer. Be sure to select one that won't turn yellow as it ages.

Head

Glue four 24-inch lengths together end to end. To make the angel's face, roll a shallow grape roll with this 96-inch length.

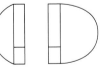

Repeat to make a deeper grape roll with another 96-inch length. Spread glue on the inside of each grape roll and allow it to dry. Then glue the two grape rolls together, matching the seams carefully. Allow the glue to dry.

Neck

Roll an 8-inch tight circle and glue it to the bottom of the head, over the area where the seams on the grape rolls meet.

Sleeves *(make two)*

Glue three 24-inch lengths of ⅜-inch-wide paper together end to end. Roll a tight circle with this 72-inch length and shape it into a 2½-inch-long cone with a rounded end. Using a toothpick, spread glue on the inner surface and allow it to dry.

Body

Glue seven 24-inch lengths of ⅜-inch-wide paper together end to end. Roll the 168-inch length into a tight circle and shape it just as you shaped the sleeve, but make this cone 4 inches long. Spread glue on the inner surface and allow it to dry.

Hands *(make two)*

The teardrop hands are made with loose circles that are too large to fit in a mold on the quilling/designer board, so you must use a special technique to shape them. Roll a 12-inch length of paper, let it open into a loose circle ½ inch in diameter, and place it on your quilling work board. Using one pointed end of a pair of tweezers, pull the center of the circle to the seam on its outer edge. Grip the gathered paper coils in the tweezers and pinch the opposite end of the loose circle to a point. Then dip the gathered coils between the points of the tweezers into glue and place the teardrop back on the plastic-covered quilling work board. When the glue has dried, the teardrop may be stuck to the plastic. Carefully loosen it with your needle tool and trim away any excess glue.

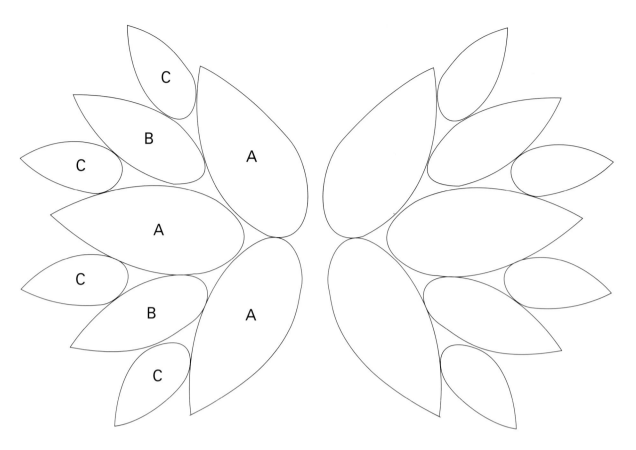

Wing Sections *(make four)*

As you can see in the photo of the angels, each wing is made up of two identical sections that are slightly offset before they're glued together. You'll start by filling in each of the two wing-section patterns twice. To make the teardrops in each section, start by using the same technique you used to make the hands to create:

    A. three 48-inch loose circles, 1¼ inch in diameter

    B. two 36-inch loose circles, 1 inch in diameter

    C. four 24-inch loose circles, ¾ inch in diameter

Shape the loose circles into teardrops and glue as before. Using the patterns, position and glue the shapes together to make four wing sections. Trim away any excess glue when it has dried.

Hair

Roll approximately seventy 1½-inch loose circles, varying their diameters from about ⅛ inch to ¼ inch. Allow the glue to dry.

Assembly

Position the body with the seam in back. Then take a look at the assembled angel (shown at the right). Flatten each sleeve slightly, positioning the seam on one flattened side. Using the photo as a guide, glue the sleeves to the body, with their seams facing inward. Allow the glue to dry.

Holding the two sections together, position them against the back of the angel. Check to see that one section fits behind the sleeve and the other section rests just at the center of the angel's back. Make adjustments as necessary; then glue the sections together. Adjust the remaining two sections in the same fashion before gluing them together to make the other wing.

To attach the assembled wings, first apply small amounts of glue to the angel's back, beneath the neck and on the backs of the sleeves. Then, using the photo as a guide, carefully press the wings in place, checking to see that they're level and flat.

When the angel is dry, glue the hair curls in place, starting between the wings at the back of the head. Be sure to glue the curls with their seam sides facing down and to position them at various angles.

Halo and Bow

To make the halo, glue a short length of gold quill trim into an open circle. Glue this circle to the hair, with its seam side to the back. To make the knot in the bow, roll an 8-inch tight circle from gold quill trim. Next, glue a 2½-inch length of gold quill trim into an open circle. To shape the circle into two loops, apply a small amount of glue to the inner surface, at the seam, and press the circle together at that point. Glue the knot between the two loops. Make the streamers by gluing two 4½-inch lengths of gold quill trim, each trimmed to an angle, to the back of the bow. Glue the bow to the body. Also glue the streamers' trimmed ends and centers to the body.

Hanger (optional)

Make a loop with 6 inches of gold cord, tying its ends together. Using tweezers, dip the knot in glue and press it into a curl at the top of the head.

Finishing

When all the glue is dry, apply five to six coats of clear acrylic spray sealer, allowing each coat to dry before applying the next.

Glue the head and neck in place next. Then glue the teardrop hands inside the sleeves, close to the body. Allow the glue to dry.

Now you must attach the wings. As you can see in the photo above, the wing sections are first glued together in offset pairs. Then each pair is glued to the back of the angel so that the front sections, which have a gap between them, tuck neatly behind the sleeves, and the back sections meet in the center of the angel's back.

To make the offset wings, first place one wing section on a flat surface, with its glued side (or back surface) up. Position a matching section on top of it, with its glued side down. Now pull the upper section to one side by ½ to ¾ of an inch so that the two large teardrops (A) on its inner edge overlap the two large teardrops (A) on the section beneath.

White-on-White Wedding Border

Why should an heirloom wedding photograph spend its life hidden within the pages of an album, when it can look so lovely in a carefully quilled frame?

Tips

- Use ⅛-inch-wide bright white paper unless another width or color is specified. You'll need green parchment paper for the leaves and stems.
- The oval in the mat board shown is 4½ inches by 6 inches.
- A ¼-inch hole punch and a punch that makes heart shapes, both available from quilling suppliers, come in handy for this project, although you can cut these tiny shapes by hand if you like.

Filigree Border

Roll approximately forty 3-inch C scrolls. Arrange these scrolls around the oval opening in the mat and glue them in place.

Roses (*make four*)

Start by reviewing the section on curled flowers (see page 14). Then, for each rose, make nine curled petals, using ½-inch lengths of ⅜-inch-wide paper. Cut one ⅜-inch square of paper and glue five petals onto it in a circle so that the curls are barely touching. Arrange the remaining four petals, also in a circle, inside the others. Using a ¼-inch hole punch, make seven to nine circles for the center of each rose. Roll one circle into a tube and gently curl the others on a quilling tool. Fill the center of the rose with tacky glue. Arrange the curled circles in the glue, press the tube into the center, and allow the glue to dry.

Fringed Flowers (*make four*)

Make four fringed flowers, using 6-inch lengths of fringed ¼-inch-wide paper.

Fringed Flowers with Centers
(*make two*)

To make each flower, first fringe a 3-inch length of ⅜-inch-wide paper; then glue a 3-inch length of ⅛-inch-wide paper to one end. Starting with the narrower paper, roll the length into a tight circle and spread the fringes as shown.

Forget-Me-Nots (make four)

Using a 1/4-inch hole punch, make five circles for each flower. Apply a medium-size dot of tacky glue to one circle and arrange the remaining four circles in the glue, overlapping them slightly. Roll a 1/2-inch tight circle with 1/16-inch-wide paper and press it into the center.

Fringed Leaves (make eight)

Using green parchment paper, cut each leaf shape, crease the center, and use scissors to fringe the edges.

Marquise Leaves (make eight)

Using green parchment paper, make eight marquise leaves.

Buds with Leaves (make two)

For each bud, first fold a 1 1/2-inch length of green parchment paper in half. Trim each end at an angle and curl each one as shown. Roll a 3-inch teardrop bud and glue its rounded end in the fold. Next, roll two 3-inch teardrop leaves from green parchment paper. Using the illustration as a guide, glue the leaves and bud together.

Teardrop Flowers (make four)

For each flower, roll a 1 1/2-inch tight circle and five 1 1/2-inch teardrops. Glue these together as shown in the illustration.

Bridal Bow

Fold a two-loop bow in the center of a 12-inch length of paper and glue the loops to maintain the bow shape. Use your fingernail to gently curve the streamers.

Carnation for Bow

Punch out one small circle and several small heart shapes. Apply a bit of glue to the circle and arrange a circle of heart shapes in the glue, with their points facing in. Crease a few more hearts and press them into the glue in the center of the circle.

Assembly

Using the photo as a guide, glue the bow directly on top of a C scroll. When the glue has dried, glue the carnation into the center of the bow.

Using the illustration as a guide, position and glue the roses, fringed flowers, fringed leaves, forget-me-nots, and buds.

To make the four stems, use 1 1/2-inch lengths of green parchment paper. Add two 1 1/2-inch loose scrolls to each one. Glue the stems in place, adding two marquise leaves to the base of each one and a teardrop flower to the tip.

Filigree Medallion

This distinctive quilled medallion has all sorts of decorative possibilities. Display it proudly in a frame; feature it on your Christmas tree each year; or reduce the design, make smaller shapes, and add the medallion to a handmade greeting card.

Tips

- Use ⅛-inch-wide paper throughout.
- When you make the eccentric shapes, use the second largest mold on the quilling/designer board for the 8-inch lengths and the third largest mold for the 12-inch lengths.
- Before you begin, trace the half-pattern provided. Then flip the tracing over, align it with the half-pattern in the book, and trace over both to make a complete pattern.

Making the Grape Rolls

Roll one crimson 24-inch grape roll, twelve crimson 6-inch grape rolls, and twelve crimson 4-inch grape rolls.

Making the Eccentric Shapes

First take a close look at the pattern. The dot inside each eccentric shape represents the "center" of the original loose circle. As you make each of these eccentric shapes, be sure to position its center as indicated.

Make the following shapes:

- six bright white 8-inch eccentric loose circles
- six bright white 12-inch eccentric loose circles
- twelve bright white 12-inch eccentric teardrops
- twelve bright white 12-inch eccentric fans

Assembly

Assemble the medallion by starting with the shapes at the center and working outward toward the pattern's edges. When the medallion is assembled, glue it to your background.

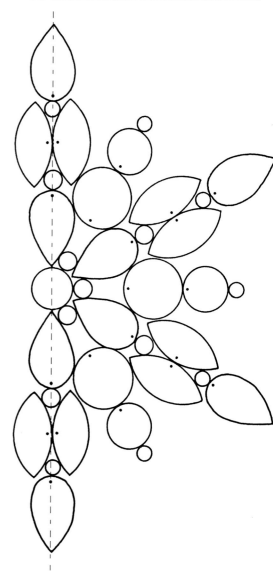

Irises

*Strikingly bold in color, this wonderful grouping of quilled
irises is layered and rounded to add visual depth.*

Tips

- Use narrow paper unless another width is specified.
- Many of the petals must be rounded and shaped after you've made them and the glue has dried. Just place the petal in the palm of one hand, with its front surface facing down, and gently press it with the fingers of the other hand.

Yellow Iris *(lower left of design)*

Fill in the six petal patterns with yellow 3-inch marquises. Gently round the larger petals.

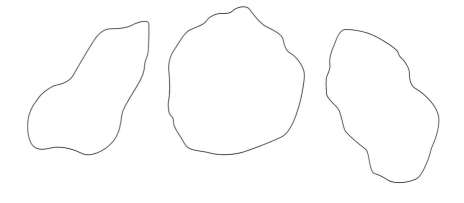

Glue the six petals together, using the illustration and photo as guides. (Ignore the dotted line in the pattern for now.)

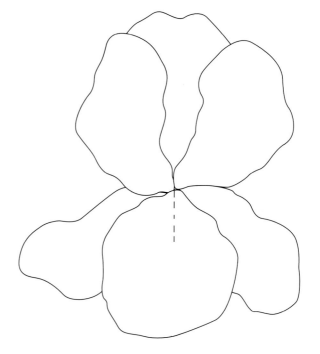

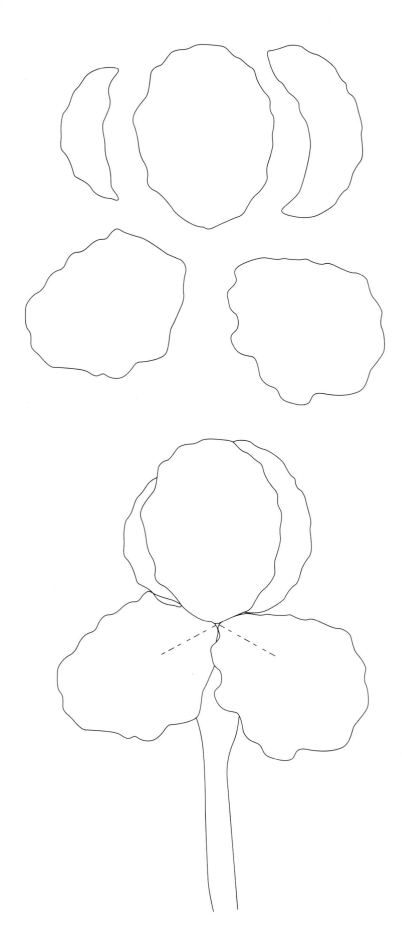

Yellow Iris and Stem (*upper right of design*)

Fill in the five petal patterns with yellow 3-inch marquises. Then gently round each petal.

To make the stem, fill in the pattern outline with green 4-inch marquises. Using the pattern as a guide, glue the petals together, overlapping them as shown. Glue the stem to the base of the flower.

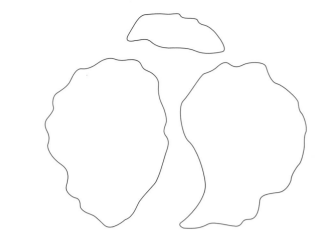

Lavender Iris *(lower right of design)*

Fill in the six petal patterns with lavender 3-inch marquises. Gently round the petals as before.

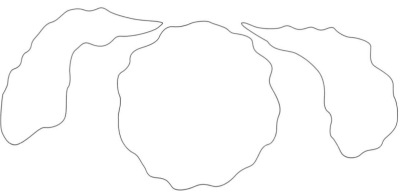

Assemble the petals as shown in the illustration.

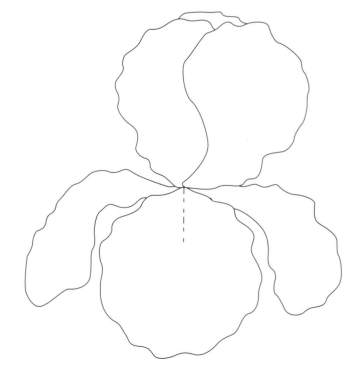

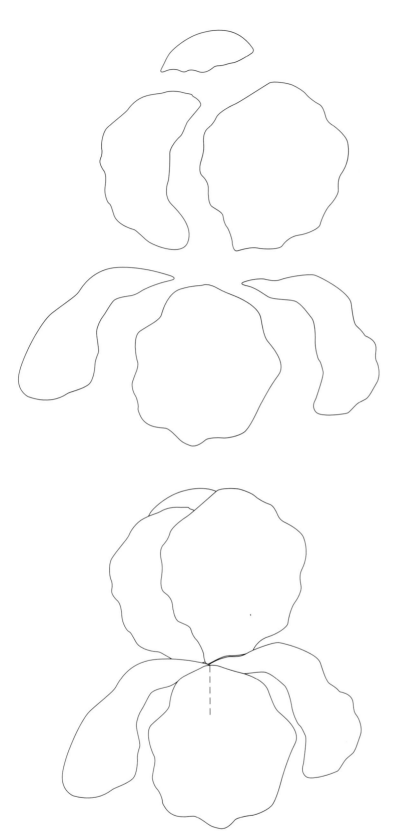

Lavender Iris *(upper left of design)*

Fill in the six petal patterns with lavender 3-inch marquises, shape the petals, and assemble as shown.

Purple Iris

Fill in the marquise outlines within each petal pattern with dark purple 3-inch marquises. Then fill in the remaining portions of the petals with purple 3-inch marquises. Round the petals and assemble as shown.

Iris Beards *(make six)*

To make a beard for each lavender iris and for the purple iris, first cut two of pattern A from yellow ⅜-inch-wide paper. Crease each piece down the center and cut fringes along both edges. Curl the fringes slightly upward and separate some as well. Glue the two fringed pieces A together, one on top of the other. Next, refer to the assembly patterns for these flowers. Using the dotted lines in these patterns as placement guides, glue the beards to the petals.

To make a beard for each yellow iris (the upper iris has two), cut two of pattern A from yellow ⅜-inch-wide paper and two of pattern B from gold ⅜-inch-wide paper. Crease, fringe, and glue together the A shapes as before and glue them to the iris at the dotted pattern lines. Fringe one edge of each gold shape, curl the fringes upward, and glue one shape on each side of the yellow beard, just beneath it.

Buds

(make two)

Fill in the bud pattern with yellow 3-inch marquises and the two calyx patterns with green 3-inch marquises. Glue the calyxes on top of the bud, overlapping them slightly as shown. To make the short stem, glue together several green 3-inch marquises; then glue the stem to the bud.

Front Layer of Leaves

Take a good look at the leaf patterns and the photo on page 59. As you can see in the photo, I chose to elevate my mat and tuck both layers of leaves under it. If you'd like to do the same, just elongate each leaf slightly. If you follow the patterns lines provided, your leaves will butt up against the edge of the mat.

Fill in the four pattern outlines with green marquises, varying the paper lengths from 3 inches for the upper shapes to 6 or 8 inches for the shapes at the bottom.

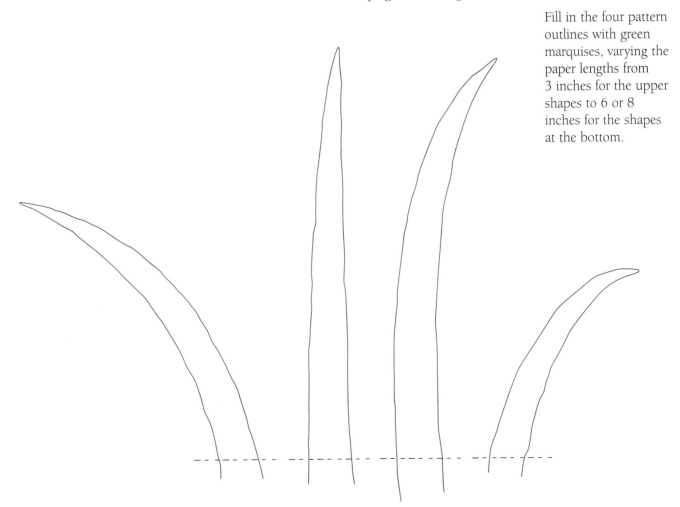

Lower Layer of Leaves

Make these leaves just as you made those in the upper layer. (Don't forget to enlarge the pattern first!)

Assembly

Using the photo as a guide, arrange the lower layer of leaves first, overlapping them as necessary. Glue them in place. Then position and glue the flowers and buds. Finally, add the four front leaves.

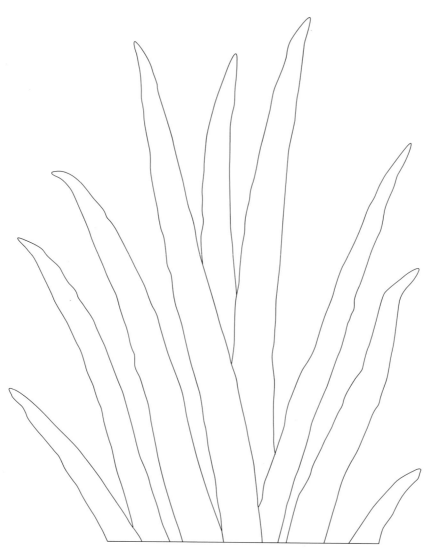

Enlarge by 200%

A

Gallery

The outstanding designs in this section represent some of the finest contemporary quillwork in existence. What makes these pieces so special? They're all skillfully executed, of course, but the magnificent quillers who created them have added qualities far more important than technical proficiency. Look closely at the photos, and you'll understand what those qualities are: dedication, love, and vision. Dedication to the craft of quilling, love of the creative quilling process, and distinctly unique visions of the world.

Let these wonderful designs inspire you. Let them encourage you to try new techniques and create your own designs. And remember that every one of the superb quillers whose work appears here once was a beginner just like you!

St. John (the eagle) and St. Luke (the calf)
Lesley Davies

These stunning quilled pieces are carefully created replicas of designs in the Book of Kells, an eighth-century illuminated manuscript of the Gospels. The original, produced at the monastery of Kells in County Meath, Ireland, is now kept at Trinity College Library in Dublin.

Sampler
Margaret Haigh

The characters, trees, people, animals, birds, and border patterns in this ornate
design are typical of those found in eighteenth- and nineteenth-century embroidered
samplers. Notice how many different quilling techniques the artist has used.

Swimming Fish
Margaret Haigh

An unusual three-dimensional design,
this leaping fish was first quilled on
a modeled form and then removed and
secured in an upright position with a covered wire.
The swirled paper around it was made by gluing
lengths of quilling paper together at each end
and then twisting the lengths to shape them.

Japanese Lady
Margaret Haigh

*To achieve depth in this lovely design,
the artist quilled the graceful lady's figure
on a low-relief modeled form,
added pegs behind the bridge,
and layered the blossoms to create bushes.*

Australian Native Elderberry
Jean Woolston-Hamey

Also known as the "honey bush," this large shrub
grows up to 12 feet in height. In the spring,
the plant is covered with a profusion of
small, white, starlike flowers that produce
a strong, sweet aroma. A shy native plant,
the elderberry grows deep in the rain forests
of Australia and in quiet, open forests.

Cathedral Window

Helen Hartley

This magnificent piece, inspired by the Rose Window
in the north transept of Notre Dame Cathedral,
looks almost exactly like real stained glass.
The artist, who also hand-shaped the wood trim
that separates and encircles the quilled arms of the design,
chose her paper colors with great care.

Papyrus Blossom Necklace
Naomi Geller Lipsky

Based on ancient
Egyptian jewelry designs,
this necklace includes
five quilled papyrus
blossoms and fancy jasper
alternating with
gold metal beads.
The artist has included
real gold leaf
on the perianth
of each blossom.

Etrog Box
Naomi Geller Lipsky
(Cherry box made by Mel
Turcanik)

During the Jewish harvest
holiday of Succot,
worshippers celebrated
four tree species—
the willow, palm,
myrtle, and etrog—
by singing and praying
while carrying a bundle
of leaves called a lulav
(shown at the left of the
box) and holding the
etrog, a lemon-like fruit
(shown at the right).
The etrog box is used
to protect the etrog
during its travels
back and forth from
the synagogue.
The Hebrew words
in this design,
which mean
"you rejoiced,"
were built
with gold leaf.

Sunflowers and Birds
Sandra White

———

This artist has developed an original cutout technique
to create very distinctive effects in her quillwork.
By placing a simple cutout over the quilling itself,
she not only defines each portion of the design,
but also creates design elements
such as the stems of the quilled flowers.

Lion

Jane Jenkins

A true love of wildlife is apparent
in this vivid quilled portrait of a regal lion.
The artist ensured realistic color tones by hand painting
much of the paper that she used in this design
and by carefully blending colors as she quilled.

About the Author

Malinda Johnston (front cover; pages 3, 16-30, and 58-66) lives in the scenic Ozark Mountains with her husband, Jim. She is the author of many instructional books, including *The Book of Paper Quilling* (Sterling, 1994). Malinda began quilling in the early 1970s, and her designs have appeared regularly in many craft publications. In 1973, she started her quilling manufacturing and supply company, the Lake City Craft Company, which is located in Nixa, Missouri and which serves accounts in 23 countries.

Contributing Designers

Australia

Jean Woolston-Hamey (page 73), of Coffs Harbor, New South Wales, learned to quill from her aunt five years ago and soon started to sell her quilled greeting cards. Jean has a special interest in creating quilled versions of her country's flora and is the author of *Quilling Australian Native Flowers*.

Canada

Joan Kiuru (pages 43-44), of Halifax, Nova Scotia, serves as the Canadian representative of The Quilling Guild in England and is a member of the Nova Scotia Designer Crafts Council. As well as teaching quilling workshops, Joan provides demonstrations for groups throughout Nova Scotia. She has won many ribbons for her quilling artistry in competitions at Canadian exhibitions and fairs, and her commissioned work is displayed in homes from Canada to Singapore.

Great Britain

Diane Crane (pages 34-36), a self-taught quiller who lives in London, has been teaching quilling for the past five years in adult education classes. She has a special interest in three-dimensional work and, in 1993, was awarded The Quilling Guild of England's Golden Salver—the highest award given at the Guild's Annual General Meeting.

Lesley Davies (pages 3 and 69), of Hull, learned to quill 12 years ago. She is a member of the Quilling Guild of England and has been its Treasurer as well. Lesley, who is also a calligrapher and who has a special interest in Celtic art, is currently quilling the two remaining evangelists from the *Book of Kells: St. Matthew* (the man) and *St. Mark* (the lion). Her quilled *St. John* won the Quilling Guild's first place award for framed quilling in 1993.

Margaret Haigh (pages 70-72) lives in Melksham, Wiltshire. She is an expert quiller who has won the highest award given by the Quilling Guild of England at its Annual General Meeting—the Golden Salver. She is a regional representative of the Quilling Guild and conducts two annual workshops for her member group. Her *Swimming Fish* received the Rosebowl Award in 1996 and her *Japanese Lady* received the same award in 1992.

Jane Jenkins (pages 45-46 and 77) lives in Cottingham, East Yorkshire, with her husband, Paul, and daughters, Cate and Jo. Jane and Paul are founding members and Honorary Vice Presidents of the Quilling Guild of England and run a mail-order business (JJ Quilling Design). Jane, who has produced books and videos on quilling techniques, is especially interested in quilling experimentation, adaptation, and invention.

Brenda Rhodes (pages 47-49), who resides in Barnstable, Devon, taught herself to quill 15 years ago. Since that time, she has given numerous quilling workshops and demonstrations and has appeared in a craft-oriented television series. Brenda is especially interested in the history of paper rolling and in the neat finish that huskings lend to quilled work.

The Netherlands

Trees Tra (pages 30-31), owner of Treart Hobby in Vught, has been quilling since 1972. She has written numerous books on a variety of paper-craft topics, including the art of quilling. Trees says that she loves paper and cannot imagine a world without it.

Republic of South Africa

Hilary Bird (pages 32-33) lives in Sarnia, where she owns a quilling-supply business, Paper Magic. Hilary was instantly captivated by quilling when she first came across it several years ago. She has since spread her knowledge of this craft around the country through her talks, demonstrations, workshops, magazine articles, and television appearances.

United States

Rita Anderson (page 37) fell in love with quilling 12 years ago. For the past ten years, she has owned her own business, Creative Quilling, in Toms River, New Jersey, and her designs appear in three or four juried shows each year. Rita says she's always been fascinated by how different one quilled design can be from another.

Patricia Caputo (pages 56-57), of Enfield, Connecticut, serves as a representative to the Quilling Guild and writes a newsletter, *Quill America,* for its United States members. Her business, Whimsiquills, specializes in quilling shadow boxes and frames. Patricia's work is sold nationwide and in many foreign countries.

Toni Christenson (pages 3 and 53-55) has been quilling for more than 20 years. In 1993, she was invited to design an angel for the White House, and her work is now part of the permanent collection there. Each year, Toni, who is legally blind and who does most of her quilling by touch, designs at least a dozen new angels, and she now has one to represent each state. Her business, TLC Crafts, is located near Bandera, Texas.

Helen Hartley (page 74), who retired from Motorola eight years ago and moved to Jerome, Arizona, is an entirely self-taught quiller. She started out ten years ago by making Christmas-tree ornaments, but now designs and creates a wide range of impressive quillwork, from Pennsylvania Dutch designs to the ornate "window" displayed in this book.

Naomi Geller Lipsky (page 75) is a freelance decorative artist who lives in Rochester, Minnesota. She is an active member of SEMVA (Southeast Minnesota Visual Artists) and is on the Board of Directors of Pomegranate Guild of Judaic Needlework. Her quillwork appears in juried shows each year and is also privately commissioned.

Eileen Maddox (pages 3 and 40-42), who lives in Grandview, Missouri, is an expert quilter and quilt designer as well as paper quiller. Eileen also enjoys graphic designing with her computer. She participates in six craft fairs each year, where she presents quilling and soft fabric crafts.

Guy and **Lura Silvernail** (pages 49-52) learned quilling together in a series of classes they took in 1973. Since that time, they have started their own business (Silvernail Crafts) and spend half of each year teaching quilling in Lady Lake, Florida and the other half teaching in Syracuse, New York. The Silvernails specialize in quilled bird designs.

Bobbye Singer (pages 38-39) has been quilling for 15 years and is an accomplished instructor as well. She participates in three shows each year, and her work is available in local galleries. Bobbye's business, Quill You Be Mine, which she runs from her home in Passaic Park, New Jersey, specializes in wedding and birth announcements.

Sandra White (page 76), who lives in Alton, New Hampshire, taught herself the art of quilling in 1973 and it has since become the main focus of her life. She owns her own business, Quilling by Sandra, and also sells her work through stores, galleries, and the League of New Hampshire Craftsmen. She especially enjoys combining her love of nature with her love of quilling.

Acknowledgments

I'm very grateful to the contributing designers for their generosity in sharing the fantastic designs in this book. It's been a real pleasure working with them all. Special thanks also to editor Chris Rich (Lark Books, Asheville, NC), photographer Evan Bracken (Light Reflections, Hendersonville, NC), and art director Elaine Thompson (Lark Books, Asheville, NC).

For information on the Quilling Guild, contact Malinda Johnston, P.O. Box 2009, Nixa, MO 65714.

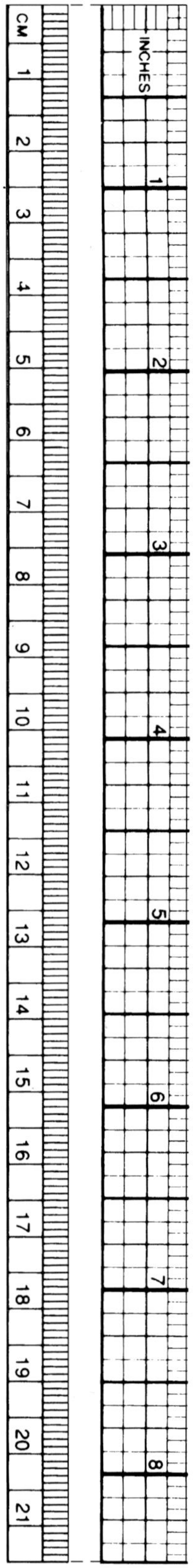

Metric Conversions

Inches	CM
⅛	0.3
¼	0.6
⅜	1.0
½	1.3
⅝	1.6
¾	1.9
⅞	2.2
1	2.5
1¼	3.2
1½	3.8
1¾	4.4
2	5.1
2½	6.4
3	7.6
3½	8.9
4	10.2
4½	11.4
5	12.7
6	15.2
7	17.8
8	20.3
9	22.9
10	25.4
11	27.9
12	30.5
13	33.0
14	35.6
15	38.1
16	40.6
17	43.2
18	45.7
19	48.3
20	50.8
21	53.3
22	55.9
23	58.4
24	61.0
25	63.5
26	66.0
27	68.6
28	71.1
29	73.7
30	76.2
31	78.7
32	81.3
33	83.8
34	86.4
35	88.9
36	91.4
37	94.0
38	96.5
39	99.1
40	101.6
41	104.1
42	106.7
43	109.2
44	111.8
45	114.3
46	116.8
47	119.4
48	121.9
49	124.5
50	127.0

Index